Beef and Braised Catfish, as wel... modernized like Lemongrass Chi... Wings, and Bò Kho "Birria" Tacos. And, no surprise, you'll find plenty of soups, such as Bitter Melon Soup, Spicy Beef Noodles, and Phở. Let's not forget the chapters on entertaining, essential sauces and condiments, and even desserts, including Soy Pudding with Ginger Syrup and Vietnamese Banana Fritters. Don't know where to begin? Tuệ includes a guide to Vietnamese pantry ingredients and menu pairings to get you started.

Whether you're among the legions of adoring fans of @TwayDaBae or an avid home cook interested in learning a new cuisine, you're bound to fall in love with the vibrant flavors that define Vietnamese cooking.

Tuệ is a culinary force whose evolution I've been honored to witness as a friend and collaborator over the years. Her debut cookbook, Đi Ăn, is as dynamic, soulful, and fiery as she is, and I can't wait for the world to discover her bold flavors and story of resilience."

—Jing Gao, founder of Fly By Jing and author of *The Book of Sichuan Chili Crisp*

"Đi Ăn is a tasty adventure that brings a fresh, modern take on traditional Vietnamese cuisine. Dish after dish, it's all hits and no misses."

—Adrian Per, film director

Dian

Di Ăn

The SALTY, SOUR, SWEET & SPICY FLAVORS of VIETNAMESE COOKING with TWAYDABAE

Tuệ Nguyễn

Photography by Andrew Bui

SIMON
ELEMENT

New York London Toronto Sydney New Delhi

For Ree

CONT

INTRODUCTION

X

~~~~~~~~~~~~~~~~~~~~~~~~~~~~~~~~~~~~~~~

CLASSICS

25

~~~~~~~~~~~~~~~~~~~~~~~~~~~~~~~~~~~~~~~

~~~~~~~~~~~~~~~~~~~~

Introduction

~~~~~~

My relationship with food is complex. It is
intimate and purposeful, sometimes challenging
but more often than not, rewarding. I'm proud
of how far I've come. I immigrated to the
United States when I was eight years old. My
parents enrolled me in school right away and
I found making friends to be very difficult. I
didn't know how to read or speak English. The
customs and cultural practices of living in
America were all new to me, but I picked them
up over time. I learned English by watching a
lot of TV, especially *SpongeBob SquarePants*
and *Anthony Bourdain: No Reservations*. I also
read a lot of books even when I didn't know
what the words meant. I read them out loud to

practice speaking English. Eventually, I made my way through *A Series of Unfortunate Events* by Lemony Snicket and piles of mystery books. After that, pursuing a career in food wasn't always easy with parents who didn't support what I wanted to do.

In high school, my parents wanted me to become a nurse, so my goal was to go to nursing school. Senior year came around and when everyone else was sending off their college applications, I felt hesitation all the way down in my gut about nursing school. It felt like the wrong decision for me, so I didn't go. I knew I had to do something, so I asked myself, "What do I really like doing?" Fam, the answer was: I love to eat. I didn't know how to cook because my mom hated having people in her kitchen. I decided to go to culinary school because it was something that genuinely excited me. Even though my mom didn't teach me how to cook, she taught me what good food tastes like through her dishes. When I cook, the only approval I need is from her.

Once I finished culinary school, my first few jobs in the food industry didn't pay very much and I was surrounded by a lot of toxic masculinity and egos in the kitchen. Being a chef is my career, but cooking is the passion that fueled my self-actualization. I was able to discover who I am in this world through food. Food has allowed me to express myself through flavors and presentations, every dish as concise and purposeful as its creator. I attribute the inspiration for my dishes back to my culture, as I have always placed Vietnamese heritage at the very forefront of everything I do in my career. I am honored to be a vessel for the people who look like me, and who resonate with my story. I can only hope that I continue to do so. In this moment, I am proud I am able to support myself and my family by doing what I really enjoy: cooking and sharing food. My internet handle, @TwayDaBae, stemmed from my friend Gabe in high school. His username at the time was "gabethebabe," and I thought that it was a catchy naming convention. I chose to start accounts on TikTok and YouTube because those were (and still are) the platforms that I use the most to consume content.

My mom's classic Vietnamese cooking has inspired me heavily as a chef and I credit her influence throughout this cookbook. In Vietnam, she had her own hair salon and when she immigrated to the United States, she worked as a nail technician. So how did she become a great cook? When you get married in Vietnam, the bride goes to live with the groom's family to cook for them. To earn their acceptance, she had to find her own way around the kitchen. And the rest is history! She has always been into beauty as her profession, but I found the beauty in her homemade food, in spite of our early clashes over my career choices. I honor her and her hardworking hands that brought me here. I've also always been responsible for taking care of my younger sister ever since she was born. She is a huge part of what has inspired me to create this cookbook, so shout-out to her! Writing this collection feels extra special because I look at these recipes as something I can pass down to her.

Vietnamese flavors are bold: a web of salty, sour, sweet, and spicy. Fish sauce is a common flavor enhancer over a salt shaker, while lemongrass, garlic, shallots, and chili peppers add aromatic pungency. We're not shy when it comes to fresh herbs and vegetables, either. Mint, cilantro, and crunchy lettuces are ever present. My goal has always been to show the world how amazing my Vietnamese culture is; that's why I make Vietnamese cooking videos, have a Vietnamese restaurant, and wrote this cookbook filled with Vietnamese recipes. Organizing group trips to Vietnam is the ultimate way for me to educate and immerse people in the culture I love so much. Imagine the constant honking of motorbikes and street vendors hawking their wares, while the smell of delicious Vietnamese street food wafts through the air. The traffic can be insane. Among the hubbub, cars and buses compete for space on the roads, too. It's chaotic but all part of the adventure of exploring this dynamic and exciting country. All these sensations of Vietnam are now distilled in my pop-up hits like Cánh Gà Chiên Nước Mắm (page 69) and Cháo Gà (page 102). I am determined to stay true to myself and don't water my menus down, never ever shying away from the scent of durian.

I understand that the technicalities of cooking can be intimidating, especially when you're just starting out. This cookbook encourages you to expand your horizons, whether it be in your palate or skill set. Since I've always believed that food is an opportunity for connection, I hope that these recipes instill the same sense of excitement and happiness when it all comes together, whether you're making it for yourself or your loved ones. As you go through this cookbook, you'll find simplified recipes that still pack the bold flavors that encompass the essence of the Vietnamese dishes I know and love. I believe in accessibility, in the knowledge that anyone and everyone can learn how to cook, whether you're a seasoned chef or a food lover just learning how to hone your cooking skills.

This cookbook is the embodiment of who I was, who I am, and who I am yet to be. I have put my heart and soul into these recipes, giving you a glimpse of my journey—not just as a chef but as an individual. I hope you see the person that I was as well as who I am continuing to become. These recipes tell a story.

One of nostalgia: depicting flavors and tastes of Vietnam, the practices that I grew up with and will honor for the rest of my life.

One of love: for appreciating the passion that has brought me to incredible heights and the feeling that washes over me when someone takes their first bite of my food.

One of redemption: for the girl who once upon a time didn't have a sense of direction, who is now leading an international community of food enthusiasts.

This book is the culmination of every pivotal moment of my life and I'm grateful for the opportunity to share it with you.

Vietnamese
Pantry   Items

~~~~~~

Broken rice is a type of rice that is broken into small pieces during the milling process. It became popular in Vietnam due to its affordability and practicality. It is the base of a dish called Cơm Tấm (page 53), in which the broken rice is served, typically, with grilled pork, a fried egg, pickled vegetables, and fish sauce. Today, cơm tấm is a ubiquitous dish in Vietnamese cuisine and is enjoyed by Vietnamese communities around the world. The dish has become an important part of Vietnam's culinary culture and is a testament to the resourcefulness of Vietnamese cooks in transforming a humble ingredient into a beloved dish.

Chinese sausage refers to the many different kinds of sausages originating from China. They are usually categorized into two kinds: liver-based sausage and red mixed-pork sausage. I prefer the latter, lap cheong, in my Viral Fried Rice (page 76). When you fry it up, it's sweet and full of umami.

Coconut milk is a creamy liquid that is extracted from grated coconut flesh. It's an essential ingredient in Vietnamese cuisine, used in a variety of dishes, from curries to soups to desserts. It adds a rich, nutty flavor and creamy texture to dishes. To store it, simply keep it in an airtight container in the refrigerator for up to a few days or freeze it for longer storage. Before using, give it a good stir or shake, as it can separate and solidify at lower temperatures.

Fish sauce is a pungent, salty condiment made by fermenting fish, typically anchovies, with salt. It's a key ingredient in Vietnamese cuisine, where it's used in everything from marinades and dipping sauces to soups and stir-fries. A lot of my recipes have fish sauce, so make sure to add this to your pantry before you start cooking. The sauce adds a deep umami flavor to dishes and is often used in place of salt to season food. You can find fish sauce in most Asian grocery stores. When shopping for fish sauce, look for one that's made with high-quality fish and has a deep, amber color. Check the label; it should only have two ingredients: anchovies and salt (like Red Boat Fish Sauce)! Avoid fish sauces that have added preservatives or artificial flavors. To store fish sauce, keep it in a cool dark place, like a pantry or cupboard. Once opened, it can be stored at room temperature, but keeping it in the fridge will prolong its shelf life.

Herbs are a vital part of Vietnamese cooking. All of the herbs here can be piled high on a side plate and enjoyed with Bánh Xèo (page 50), all my braises, and soups.

Fish mint, or diếp cá, is an herb known for its cooling sensation and slight fishy flavor when you chew it. Try it in my Bún Chả (page 46) and Pickled Garlic Shrimp Ceviche (page 88). When you can't source it, plain fresh mint leaves are suitable.

Lemon balm, or kinh giới, is an aromatic from the mint family that is grown for its mildly lemon-scented leaves.

Mint is a widely known and generally available fresh herb. It has a more distinct, numbing flavor in comparison to its spearmint counterpart.

Perilla leaf, or tía tô, is an intense aromatic from the mint family. Its flavor is somewhere between mint and basil. Perilla is a common ingredient in Korea, Japan, Thailand, and, of course, Vietnam. Try it with seafood and salads.

Rice paddy herb, or ngò ôm, tastes like a cross between earthy cumin and citrus. Unlike the other herbs on this list, you can eat the soft stems. I chop them into 1-inch sections for Canh Chua (page 126).

Sawtooth herb, or ngò gai, is sometimes referred to as a stronger, sturdier alternative to cilantro. They are both part of the *Apiaceae* family but are not the same plant. You might see sawtooth herb labeled as culantro or recao in Latin American grocery stores.

Spearmint, or húng lũi, is an herb with a light, vaguely sweet flavor when compared to plain fresh mint leaves.

Thai basil, or húng quế, is a native basil to Southeast Asia.

Ngò Gai - Sawtooth Herb

Tiá Tô - Perilla Leaf

Kinh Giới - Lemon Balm

Húng Quế - Thai Basil

Ngò Ôm - Rice Paddy Herb

Húng Cây - Mint

Rau Răm - Viet Coriander

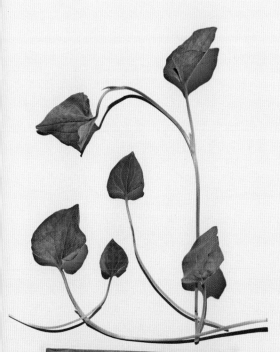

Diếp Cá - Fish Mint Herb

Húng Lũi - Spearmint

When you compare it to sweet grocery store basil, Thai basil is hardier and can withstand the high temperatures of phở broth. Its anise flavor is also stronger. I prefer Thai basil in my Lemongrass Chili Oil Noodles (page 80) and Pickled Garlic Shrimp Ceviche (page 88). But if you can't locate any at your local Asian grocery store, regular sweet basil leaves are a good substitute.

Vietnamese coriander, or rau răm, is a member of the knotweed family. Its flavor is simultaneously sweet, grassy, peppery, and sour. I love it in Gỏi Gà (page 107). If you have trouble finding it, fresh cilantro will be just fine.

Jasmine rice is different from other rice varieties by its distinctive fragrance, flavor, and texture. Unlike plain white rice, jasmine rice has a delicate, slightly floral aroma that is reminiscent of pandan leaves or popcorn. It also has a subtle, sweet flavor that complements savory dishes well. In terms of texture, jasmine rice is slightly sticky and tender, but not overly chewy or starchy. This makes it ideal for dishes where the rice should be a supporting element rather than the focus. Additionally, jasmine rice has a long, slender grain shape that sets it apart from other types of rice, such as short-grain sushi rice or medium-grain Arborio rice used for risotto.

Kosher salt is not Vietnamese, but I use it to support other stronger flavoring agents like fish sauce and soy sauce. I use Diamond Crystal brand in these recipes for its larger grain size and ability to stick on to proteins better. Be careful when substituting other types of salt like iodized, sea salt, or other brands of kosher salt; the grains are smaller and can lead to overly salty dishes. It's best to use less salt if you don't have kosher, and taste as you go.

Lemongrass is a fragrant herb that's commonly used in Southeast Asian cuisine, including Vietnamese cuisine. It has a lemony, slightly sweet flavor, and a distinctive aroma. You can usually find fresh lemongrass at Asian grocery stores or in the produce section of many supermarkets. When shopping for lemongrass, look for stalks that are firm and fragrant, with no signs of wilting or discoloration. You can also find dried or powdered lemongrass in many spice aisles, although fresh is preferred in my recipes. To prepare lemongrass for cooking, remove the dry outermost layer. Cut 1 inch off the end and the top 5 inches, leaving you with a tender white center that is easy to work with. It is then ready for mincing or bruising. To bruise it, keep the lemongrass whole but smash it to release its flavor, taking care not to smash it so hard that it breaks into many pieces. To store fresh lemongrass, keep it in the fridge in a plastic bag or wrapped in damp paper towels. It should keep for about 2 weeks. Alternatively, you can freeze lemongrass for up to 6 months. Simply chop it into pieces and store it in an airtight container in the freezer. When you're ready to use it, thaw and chop as needed.

Maggi seasoning is a liquid flavor enhancer, an umami bomb condiment made of hydrolyzed wheat protein. Its taste reminds me of soy sauce—but much more complex and herby. I pull out Maggi seasoning for Bò Lúc Lắc (page 32) and "The Shooketh Burger" (page 108).

MSG is short for monosodium glutamate, an all-purpose flavor booster. MSG is totally optional and nice to have around the kitchen. A little goes a long way! You can add a pinch to all stir-fries, braises, and soups in this book.

Noodles are always welcome in my kitchen. Dried varieties last forever in the pantry if you keep them in a cool, dark place. Fresh noodles are best refrigerated and used as soon as you can.

Rice vermicelli, or rice sticks, are thin, quick-cooking noodles. They're great for stir-fries, soup, and my Bún Chả (page 46). A word of warning: you should never boil them for too long or they will fall apart.

Miến are transparent noodles made from mung beans or, sometimes, sweet potatoes. They go by many names, so look on the package for "cellophane noodles," "glass noodles," "vermicelli," or "bean thread." They soak up liquids really fast and have a bouncy texture. Miến are much thinner than phở noodles and thicker than rice vermicelli.

Oyster sauce is a thick savory sauce made from oysters, soy sauce, sugar, and various seasonings. You can find oyster sauce in most supermarkets or Asian grocery stores, either in bottles or in sachets. To store, keep it in a cool, dry place, away from direct sunlight, and refrigerate after opening. It's important to note that oyster sauce is not vegetarian, as it contains oyster extracts. However, there are vegetarian versions of oyster sauce available that use mushrooms as a substitute.

Palm sugar is a natural sweetener made from the sap of palm trees. It's got this unique flavor that's a mix of caramel, butterscotch, and toffee. In Vietnamese cooking, it's often caramelized to add some sweetness to marinades, sauces, and desserts. To keep it fresh, just pop it in an airtight container at room temperature and store in a cool, dry place.

Pandan leaves, also known as screw pine leaves, are a popular herb in Vietnamese cuisine. They have a unique aroma that is both floral and nutty, with a sweet, vanilla-like flavor. Pandan leaves are commonly used in desserts, such as cakes, puddings, and sweet soups, as well as in savory dishes like rice and curries. I haven't had any luck finding fresh pandan leaves, but frozen pandan leaves should be available at most Asian grocery stores.

Rock sugar is a type of crystallized sugar used in Vietnamese cuisine to sweeten soups, stews, and marinades. You'll also see that I use it for simple syrup in desserts. It's more on the subtle sweet side and dissolves better than regular sugar. It looks clear and sparkly,

BỘT NGỌT

BÁNH PHỞ TƯƠI
Fresh Rice Stick Noodle
新鮮潮州粿條
월남쌀국수
ก๋วยเตี๋ยวเส้นเล็ก

BÁNH PHỞ - PHO RICE NOODLES

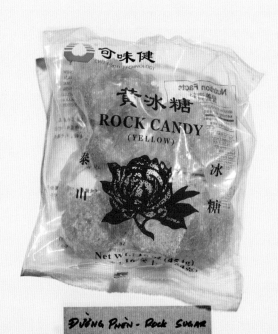

黃冰糖
ROCK CANDY
(YELLOW)

ĐƯỜNG PHÈN - ROCK SUGAR

WET
TAMARIND
酸仔糕
(SEEDLESS 無核)

QUẢ ME - TAMARIND

too! Store rock sugar in a sealed container at room temperature. To use it, add it to hot preparations and stir to dissolve it. If you can't find it, substitute an equal weight of granulated sugar.

Sambal oelek is a chili paste that originates from Indonesia. I use it to add a bit of spice to Miến Xào Cua (page 98) and Nước Mắm (page 173).

Seedless tamarind paste is a thick, tangy, and slightly sweet paste made from the pulp of the tamarind fruit. It is commonly used in Vietnamese cuisine to add a sweet-tart flavor to dishes such as soups, stews, and dipping sauces. Tamarind paste can be found at Asian grocery stores, specialty food stores, and online retailers. When you're looking for tamarind paste, it's important to check the label to be sure that it contains only tamarind pulp and no added sugar or preservatives. Double-check that you're buying seedless paste in a pressed cake, not frozen tamarind juice or "pulp." To store tamarind, keep it in an airtight container in the refrigerator for several months. You can also freeze it in small portions for longer-term storage. Despite the "seedless" description, you still need to dilute and strain it due to its fibrous texture. To use tamarind paste, break the cake up into smaller chunks, dissolve it in hot water, and strain it through a fine-mesh sieve. It is now ready to add to your dish to achieve the desired level of tartness.

Soy sauce is a key ingredient in Vietnamese cuisine, providing depth and umami flavor to many dishes. It comes in a range from light to dark varieties and can be found in most supermarkets or Asian grocery stores. For my recipes, assume I'm using an all-purpose soy sauce unless otherwise noted. Look for a high-quality product made from natural ingredients and store it in a cool, dry place away from direct sunlight. Refrigerate the bottle after opening to prolong its shelf life.

Split yellow mung beans are the peeled version of green mung beans. In Indian stores, they are labeled as moong dal. It's important you don't mix them up with the whole green beans, which are earthier and not as sweet. I use split yellow mung beans in desserts, as filling in my Chè Trôi Nước (page 204) and as a topping for Chè Ba Màu (page 214).

Sriracha is a Thai chili sauce commonly used to kick up the heat in soups and noodles, but you can pretty much use it on everything. The most popular brand in the United States is Huy Fong, also fondly known as "rooster sauce."

Recommended Tools

~~~~~~~~~~~~~~~~~~~~~~~~~~~

A *bamboo steamer* is an essential tool for making bao buns and dumplings. It's also great to have on hand for cooking any delicate foods like vegetables or fish, and perfect for reheating meals, too! A 10-inch steamer with two tiers will fit over a Dutch oven, large pot, or in a wok.

Cheesecloth is an amazing tool for straining liquids and making sachets of herbs or spices. When you need to strain a liquid, layer the cheesecloth over a fine-mesh sieve over a bowl and proceed.

A *chef's knife*, a *paring knife*, and a *serrated knife* are the most important knives one should own if they're just starting to cook. My chef's knife and my paring knife get the most use when I prepare meat and vegetables.

Cooking chopsticks are longer thin chopsticks that are commonly used in Asian cuisine for cooking and serving food. They are typically made of bamboo or stainless steel and are designed to handle hot and heavy ingredients. Cooking chopsticks are versatile and can be used to stir-fry, pick up, and turn food while cooking, and even remove items from boiling water or oil.

A *saucepan* is a pan with straight sides and a long handle used for heating and cooking sauces, soups, and stews. I have a 6-inch small and 8-inch medium pan in my kitchen.

A *sauté pan* is a wide pan, similar to a skillet but deeper and with straight sides, used for sautéing and stir-frying. It often comes with a lid.

A *skillet* or *frying pan* is a flat-bottomed pan with slightly sloping sides used for frying and sautéing, as well as searing meats and vegetables at high temperatures.

A *stockpot* is a large deep pot (deeper than it is wide) used for making stocks and large-yield soups, and for boiling pasta or potatoes. Mine is an 8-quart capacity. Additionally, you'll also need a small 2-quart pot for frying and a medium 4-quart pot or Dutch oven for soups.

Tongs are my favorite tool in the kitchen because it's like an extension of my arm and it's so easy to grab food with. The only thing to watch out for is scratching the bottom of your coated pans with tongs—I opt for cooking chopsticks in those cases.

Tweezers are great for plating and little tedious work. They're not necessary but nice to have.

A *wok* is a must-have pan for any Asian kitchen, and for good reason! Its unique shape and sloping sides make cooking fast and efficient. It's perfect for stir-frying, steaming, deep-frying, and boiling. To use a wok at home, season it by rubbing oil on the surface and heating it over high heat. I give my woks a good seasoning before I first use them. Over time, if one's looking a little dry, I'll season it again. I don't follow any specific schedule; it depends on how often I use it. Once seasoned, you're ready to add your ingredients and stir-fry away! Just make sure not to overcrowd the wok, as it can cause food to steam instead of fry. When buying a wok, choose a durable material like carbon steel, and pick the right size for your needs. If you don't think you'll be using a wok that often, another alternative is a flat-bottomed wok. Its flat base doubles as a regular nonstick skillet and a wok. Plus, it works for both gas and electric stovetops. I look to Frök brand for these and love using them, too.

Suggested Menus

Listen, I know it can be hard to decide what to cook first from this book. Luckily for you, I put together a few foolproof menus to guide you through my take on Vietnamese cuisine. Some of these are from pop-up events and some are suggestions for entertaining guests in your home. Feel free to swap in other dishes to make the menus your own.

Madame Vo

In 2022, Chef Jimmy Ly of Madame Vo invited me to collaborate for a Lunar New Year celebration. Re-create my first New York City pop-up at home.

Cháo Gà / Chicken Porridge (page 102)

Gỏi Gà / Chicken Slaw (page 107)

Canh Khổ Qua / Bitter Melon Soup (page 128)

Thịt Kho / Braised Pork (page 42)

Chè Trôi Nước / Drifting Water Dessert (page 204)

Rising Chef

Rising Chef is an annual series of pop-ups hosted by the Japanese American Cultural and Community Center in Los Angeles. I was honored to be invited and highlighted with fellow upcoming LA chefs. If you couldn't get a ticket, don't worry, you can now make the dishes I made that night in your kitchen.

Chicken Clay Pot (page 100)

Miến Xào Cua / Crab Cellophane Noodles (page 98)

Vietnamese Coffee Crème Brûlée (page 112)

Chị Hai

Chị hai means "older sister," a nickname people on TikTok call me because they see me as their older sister cooking for them. Impress your friends and family with my TikTok-famous dishes.

Lemongrass Chili Oil (page 186)

Honey-Glazed Shrimp (page 67)

Bò Lúc Lắc / Shaking Beef (page 32)

Cánh Gà Chiên Nước Mắm / Fish Sauce Wings (page 69)

Xíu Mại / Pork Meatballs (page 72)

Garlic Noodles (page 78)

Lemongrass Chicken (page 66)

Kem Bơ / Avocado Mousse (page 202)

Brunch

Hosting brunch at your house? I got you. Pro tip: Prep everything the day before so you don't have to spend the whole morning over the stove.

Garlic Green Beans (page 30)

Crispy Pork Belly (page 56)

Grilled Scallops (page 150)

Crab Fried Rice (page 44)

Canh Chua / Vietnamese Sour Soup (page 126)

Dinner party

Go all out for your loved ones with some of my greatest hits.

Shrimp Toast (page 147)
BBQ Duck Buns (page 158)
Kevin's Phở (page 138)

Cua Rang Me / Tamarind Crab Legs (page 161)

Chè Thái / Mixed Fruit Cocktail Dessert (page 213)

I'm bombarded by nostalgia whenever I think about wha

food with bonding. It was important for my whole

feels so warm and full when I remember the classic meal

my grandpa's house. We'd sit on the floor because ther

food. I was always on rice duty, meaning I would scoo

My dad's oldest sister, my aunty, was the best cook in

at least two, maybe three proteins

As adults, we tend t

ood meant to me growing up. My brain associates

family to sit down and eat together. My heart

my family would prepare. Dinner would always be at

asn't a table big enough for all of us and the

he rice and make sure everyone had their own bowl.

he house and would make everything. She cranked out

n addition to bountiful veggies and a soup.

ediscover our love for these dishes after we leave home.

classics

We're struck by an inevitable craving for warm, lovingly made food that seems to follow us wherever we go in life. With our busy grown-up schedules, it's even more special when we can sit down with family and friends for a home-cooked meal. This chapter is the embodiment of that feeling. You'll find some of my favorite classic Vietnamese dishes, including velvety soft braised pork belly, umami-rich steak, and clear tapioca dumplings that are as beautiful as they are delectable. Whether you're missing your family or want a plate full of love and flavor, these recipes will quickly become classics in your home, too.

Steamed White Rice

Prep Time: *15 minutes*
Total Time: *30 minutes*
Makes *a first course for 4*

Rice is life. I took my rice duty seriously when I was little. Every family dinner had either steamed rice or fried rice. It was my job to make sure everyone had a bowl. My grain of choice is jasmine, which is a long-grain rice originating from Southeast Asia, specifically Thailand, Cambodia, Laos, and duh, Vietnam. It is a naturally soft grain that plumps up so nicely, making it the perfect accompaniment for both old school and new school Vietnamese dishes.

1   To make the rice in a rice cooker: In the bowl of a rice cooker, wash the rice with cold water. Swish it around with your fingers and drain it. Wash again with a few more changes of water until the water runs clear. Add 2 cups cold water to the rice and swirl it slightly to level it out. Place it in the rice cooker and turn it on or choose the white rice setting. It may take 20 to 30 minutes. When it is finished, let it stand for 10 minutes more on the warm setting before serving.

2   To make the rice on the stovetop: Wash the rice as directed above and place the washed rice and $2\frac{1}{4}$ cups cold water in a medium pot. Bring it to a boil over medium-high heat, uncovered. Once boiling, reduce the heat to medium-low, cover, and steam for 12 minutes. Remove from the heat and let stand for 10 minutes. Serve warm.

2 cups **jasmine rice**

2 to $2\frac{1}{4}$ cups **cold water,** plus more for washing

In Vietnam, I watched a vendor on the side of the road make street corn. It was my first time encountering it and I remember salivating over its smells and sounds. Sizzling, roasted corn, somehow both sweet and salty, perfumed the air. I ate it kernel by kernel, savoring every last bite, and wishing it would last forever. At this exact moment, I fell in love with corn. You can experience this feeling at home! Viet street corn is a great snack or side, but make sure you don't skip the dried shrimp—it's what makes this dish special. Make sure you have everything prepped and ready to go because high-heat cooking happens very quickly.

Viet Street Corn

Prep Time: *10 minutes*

Total Time: *20 minutes*

Makes *a first course for 2*

2 ears **sweet corn**, shucked

1 cup **hot water**

¼ cup **dried shrimp**

2 tablespoons **avocado oil**

4 **scallions**, chopped

2 tablespoons **unsalted butter**

¼ cup **Fried Shallots** (page 194)

Kosher salt

1   Slice the corn kernels from the cobs and set aside. Discard the cobs.

2   In a small bowl, pour the hot water over the dried shrimp to rehydrate. Let soak for 5 minutes, then drain the shrimp.

3   Heat the avocado oil in a sauté pan over high heat until it starts to smoke, 3 to 4 minutes. Add the corn and cook, stirring, until the kernels get a little toasty color, 1 to 2 minutes. Working with one ingredient at a time, add the drained shrimp, scallions, butter, and fried shallots and cook, stirring, for 1 to 2 minutes before adding the next ingredient. Season with a pinch of salt, adding more to taste, if needed. Transfer to a bowl and serve immediately.

Garlic Green Beans

Prep Time: *15 minutes*
Total Time: *35 minutes*
Makes *a first course for 4*

Many of the recipes I will share with you are excellent main dishes for hosting a potluck or delicious weeknight dinners. But a star is only as good as its supporting actors and that's why you need to make my garlic green beans. It appears simple but when it's done well, even the pickiest eaters will be reaching for more vegetables. Garlic green beans go with pretty much everything in this book, but I've been known to make it for a midday pick-me-up snack, too. Make sure you dry the green beans thoroughly before you fry them so they don't pop in the oil and become soggy.

1 Rinse and dry the green beans well and pat dry with paper towels.

2 Line a plate with paper towels. Heat the avocado oil in a medium 4-quart pot over high heat until a green bean tossed into the oil sizzles. Working in handful-size batches, carefully flash-fry the green beans in the oil until they look slightly wrinkled, 2 to 3 minutes. Remove the beans from the oil and place on the paper towels. Be sure to wait a few minutes and let the oil come back up to high heat between batches.

3 Carefully pour all but 2 tablespoons of the avocado oil into a heatproof container. Save the reserved oil for another recipe or everyday use.

1 pound **green beans**, trimmed

1 cup **avocado oil**

4 **garlic cloves**, minced

1½ teaspoons **soy sauce**

¼ teaspoon **kosher salt**, plus more to taste

¼ teaspoon **freshly ground black pepper**, plus more to taste

4 Return the pot to medium heat, add the garlic, and cook, stirring, until golden in color, about 1 minute. Return the green beans to the pan and toss together with the garlic. Add the soy sauce, salt, and pepper and quickly toss again.

Taste a green bean and adjust the seasoning with more salt and pepper, if needed.

5 Transfer the green beans to a platter and serve hot.

Shaking Beef

BÒ LÚC LẮC

Prep Time: *1 hour*

Total Time: *1 hour 30 minutes*

Makes *a first course for 4 or main course for 2*

Shaking beef, aka bò lúc lắc, is my dad's favorite dish. Although he's not the best cook, this is his go-to meal. It never came out the way he wanted. During my junior year of high school, I decided to help him figure it out. All due credit goes to him for giving me a base to work with and giving me the green light when it tasted perfect.

I use filet mignon in this recipe. Other affordable cuts like tenderloin or chuck are great alternatives. Many recipes toss pepper and onions with the beef like fajitas. I included those veggies as optional add-ins. Be careful not to marinate the meat for too long! It makes the texture tough and it's difficult to get a good color on the sear. A platter of shaking beef is extremely hearty and savory, so make sure there are plenty of fresh toppings to balance it out. I suggest watercress, cucumber, and tomato, but you can also use sliced apples and jicama. You'll notice I use Maggi liquid seasoning, too. It's an umami-packed condiment that reminds me of soy sauce—but much more complex and herby.

(recipe continues)

2 tablespoons **granulated sugar**

2 tablespoons **oyster sauce**

2 tablespoons **Maggi liquid seasoning**

1 tablespoon **honey**

1 tablespoon **minced garlic**

1 tablespoon **sambal oelek**

½ teaspoon **sesame oil**

1 pound **filet mignon**, cut into 1-inch cubes

1 cup packed **watercress**

1 **Persian** (mini) **cucumber**, thinly sliced

6 **cherry tomatoes**, halved or 2 **Roma (plum) tomatoes**, quartered

¼ cup **avocado oil**

½ **red onion** (optional), cut into thin strips

½ **red bell pepper** (optional), thinly sliced

French fries or **Steamed White Rice** (page 26), for serving

1   In a large bowl, stir together the sugar, oyster sauce, Maggi seasoning, honey, garlic, sambal, and sesame oil. Add the beef to the bowl, mix well, and cover. Marinate at room temperature for at least 30 and up to 45 minutes, max.

2   Arrange the watercress, cucumber, and tomatoes on a serving platter. Set aside.

3   When the beef is done marinating, heat the avocado oil in a 10-inch skillet over high heat and get the pan piping hot until it starts to smoke, 3 to 4 minutes.

4   Add the beef and any marinade to the pan (along with the onion and bell pepper, if using). Let everything bubble in a single layer to develop a brown color and evaporate the marinade, about 2 minutes. Toss it all once with tongs to sear the other sides quickly and remove the pan from the heat.

5   Carefully pour the shaking beef and pan juices over the bed of watercress and veggies. Enjoy with a side of French fries or steamed white rice.

At first, cá kho was intimidating to learn because working with sugar is probably one of the most difficult things to master: it can burn so easily. I was determined to perfect a foolproof method because it is such an essential Viet dish. When you get to the caramelization stage, you're looking for a dark golden-brown color, and you need to keep stirring so everything gets melted down evenly. If you find that working with granulated sugar is too difficult because it melts too fast, try using palm sugar for its larger granules. This recipe shares a similar technique to that of Thịt Kho (page 42) and Chicken Clay Pot (page 100). The catfish is traditionally cut into steaks, but it wouldn't ruin the dish if you can only get fillets. I recommend trying different types of fish, like salmon or tuna, too.

Braised Catfish

Cá Kho

Prep Time: *1 hour 25 minutes*
Total Time: *1 hour 50 minutes*
Makes *a main course for 4*

(recipe continues)

4 **catfish steaks** or **fillets** (4 ounces each)

¼ cup **fish sauce**

¼ cup **sugar**

1 to 3 **fresh Thai bird's eye chilies** (optional), thinly sliced

¼ cup **room-temperature water**

6 **garlic cloves**, minced

2 **medium shallots**, minced

¼ cup **coconut soda**

3 **scallions**, minced

2 teaspoons **freshly ground black pepper**

Steamed White Rice (page 26), for serving

1 Place the catfish in a large bowl and drizzle on the fish sauce, 2 tablespoons of the sugar, and 1 Thai bird's eye chili (if using). Mix well, making sure each piece of catfish is coated. Cover the bowl with plastic wrap and marinate in the fridge for 30 to 45 minutes.

2 Add the remaining 2 tablespoons sugar to a medium 4-quart pot or 8-inch clay pot set over medium heat and cook, stirring, until melted. At the 2-minute mark, it will start to clump up into tan crystals and will melt again. Continue to stir occasionally until it is caramelized to a golden brown, 5 to 7 minutes. Carefully stream in the water and stir. It will harden and melt again in 2 minutes. Once it thickens into a dark brown caramel, stir in the garlic and shallots and let them sizzle undisturbed for 1 minute.

3 Add the catfish to the pot in a single layer and pour the marinade mixture over it. Cover and cook for 5 minutes. Flip the catfish and add the coconut soda to the pot. Cover and cook until the fish is thoroughly opaque, no longer pink, and tinged brown from the sugar glaze, 5 to 8 minutes.

4 Reduce the heat to medium-low. Add the scallions, black pepper, and up to 2 more Thai bird's eye chilies, if you like it spicy. Simmer undisturbed for 3 minutes longer.

5 Transfer the catfish to a large serving bowl and pour over any leftover pan juices. Serve hot with steamed white rice.

Chicken Curry

Cà Ri Gà

Prep Time: *50 minutes*

Total Time: *1 hour 50 minutes*

Makes *a first course for 4 or main course for 2*

3 **fresh lemongrass stalks**

5 tablespoons **avocado oil**

1 tablespoon **annatto seeds** (optional)

1½ pounds **bone-in, skin-on chicken parts**

2 tablespoons **fish sauce**

1 tablespoon **minced fresh ginger**

3 tablespoons **curry powder**

Cloves from 1 head **garlic**, minced

2 tablespoons **minced shallot**

2 large or 4 small **Yukon Gold potatoes**, peeled and cut into ½-inch pieces

1 large **carrot**, peeled and cut into ½-inch pieces

½ **yellow onion**, julienned

1 (13.5-ounce) can **coconut milk**

½ cup **chicken stock**

1 tablespoon **cornstarch**

Kosher salt and **freshly ground black pepper**

Fish sauce

Baguette, vermicelli noodles, or **Steamed White Rice** (page 26), for serving

Of all the curries in Vietnamese cuisine, chicken curry is one of the most well known. Since every culture has its own version of curry, you might already know how to make something like this! Cà ri gà draws its flavorful, warm, and rich flavor from Indian cuisine. However, the key difference is the sauce. In Vietnam, it's almost broth-like, which is much thinner than the curries you see in East Asian and South Asian diasporas. I recommend using dark meat because it's more tender and holds onto the curry flavor better. Plus, because of its higher fat content, it's harder to overcook compared to white meat. And if we're being honest, it just tastes better (especially the skin)! I prefer my cà ri gà with steamed white rice, but feel free to try it out with vermicelli noodles or a baguette.

1 Remove the dry, outermost layer from each lemongrass stalk. Trim the top 5 inches and 1 inch from the bottom root end, leaving you with a tender white center. Bruise the stalks with a pestle, rolling pin, or bottom of a pot. Mince 2 of the lemongrass stalks and slice the third in half lengthwise.

2   If you are not using annatto seeds, skip this oil tempering step. In a small saucepan, combine 4 tablespoons of the avocado oil and the annatto seeds and heat over medium–high heat until the oil bubbles, 1 to 2 minutes. Remove from the heat and carefully strain the oil into a heatproof container. Discard the seeds and set the oil aside.

3   Place the chicken pieces into a large bowl and sprinkle with the fish sauce, ginger, 2 tablespoons of the curry powder, 2 tablespoons of the annatto oil if using, half the garlic, half the minced lemongrass, and half the shallot. Mix it well to make sure every piece is coated. Cover the chicken with plastic wrap and let it marinate for a minimum of 30 minutes or overnight in the fridge.

4   Frying the vegetables is optional, but it helps them keep their shape when they cook with the chicken. Heat the remaining 1 tablespoon avocado oil in a 10-inch sauté pan or skillet over medium heat until it is shimmering, 2 to 3 minutes. Add the potatoes and carrot and cook, stirring, until lightly browned, 3 to 4 minutes. Transfer the vegetables to a plate.

5   To the same pot, add the yellow onion and the remaining garlic, minced lemongrass, and shallot and cook, stirring, until they start to turn translucent, 3 to 4 minutes.

6   Add the remaining 1 tablespoon curry powder and 2 tablespoons annatto or avocado oil to the pot, mix well, and scoot the aromatics to the sides. Add the marinated chicken in a single layer. Let the pieces sear undisturbed for about 3 minutes. Flip them over and cook until the chicken skin renders its fat and browns, about 3 minutes longer.

7   Stir in the coconut milk, chicken stock, vegetables, and halved lemongrass stalk. Let the curry bubble gently for about 10 minutes.

8   In a small bowl, stir 2 tablespoons water into the cornstarch to make a slurry. Pour it into the curry and stir until it starts to thicken. Let the curry cook for 10 more minutes, stirring occasionally. Adjust the seasonings to taste with salt, black pepper, and/or fish sauce. Cook until the potatoes and carrot are fork-tender, about 5 minutes longer.

9   Transfer the curry to a serving bowl. Serve hot with a baguette, vermicelli noodles, or steamed white rice.

Thịt Kho, page 42

Braised Pork

Thịt Kho

Prep Time: *55 minutes*

Total Time: *2 hours 10 minutes*

Makes *a main course for 4*

Every family has its own version of thịt kho and every family believes their version is the most superior. I completely understand the sentiment since I feel the same about mine. I hold this recipe so close to my heart because it is the most iconic humble dish in Vietnam, and it was also the first dish that I learned to cook to impress my mom. Imagine the most tender and flavorful pork belly with hard-boiled quail eggs (you can use chicken eggs if you want). I use a similar caramelizing technique for my Cá Kho (page 35) and Chicken Clay Pot (page 100) if you'd like to keep practicing. In terms of spiciness, start with 2 Thai bird's eye chilies and add more if you can handle the heat.

1 pound **skin on pork belly**, sliced into ½-inch-wide slices

4 tablespoons **light brown sugar**

4 tablespoons **fish sauce**

2 tablespoons **minced garlic**

2 tablespoons **soy sauce**

1 tablespoon **minced shallot**

½ teaspoon **kosher salt**

18 **quail eggs**

1½ teaspoons **freshly ground black pepper**

¼ cup **coconut soda** (optional)

2 to 4 **fresh Thai bird's eye chilies**, thinly sliced

4 **scallions**, thinly sliced

Steamed White Rice (page 26), for serving

1   In a large bowl, combine the pork belly, 2 tablespoons of the brown sugar, 2 tablespoons of the fish sauce, the garlic, 1 tablespoon of the soy sauce, the shallot, and salt. Mix until the pork pieces are all coated. Cover with plastic wrap and marinate for 30 minutes in the refrigerator.

2   Bring a small pot of water to a vigorous boil over high heat. Carefully lower the quail eggs into the water with a slotted spoon and cook for 4 minutes. Transfer to a bowl of cold water to cool 10 minutes. Place the quail eggs in a plastic container with some water, cover the

container, and shake the quail eggs. This will help to peel the quail eggs much more quickly, I promise! Peel the eggs and rinse gently under cold water to get rid of any bits of shell. Set aside in a bowl.

3 Remove the pork belly from the fridge and let come to room temperature for 30 minutes.

4 In a 4-quart pot, stir the remaining 2 tablespoons brown sugar over medium heat until the sugar is completely melted, 2 to 3 minutes. Carefully pour 1 tablespoon water over the sugar and stir a few times; this will make the sugar harden but don't worry, you're on the right track. In another 1 to 2 minutes the sugar will dissolve again and turn into a delicious caramel.

5 Add the pork belly with its marinade to the pot and cook, stirring a few times to coat, until the pork renders its fat, about 5 minutes. Add the remaining 2 tablespoons fish sauce, the remaining 1 tablespoon soy sauce, and the black pepper and stir once to coat the pork in the caramel sauce. Cover and cook until the pork is glazed in the sauce, about 10 minutes longer.

6 Mix in the cooked quail eggs, being careful not to break them. Add the coconut soda (if using), cover, and cook for an additional 5 minutes. Give it one more gentle stir.

7 Transfer the thịt kho to a large bowl or platter. Garnish it with the Thai bird's eye chilies and scallions. Enjoy with steamed white rice.

Crab Fried Rice

Prep Time: *10 minutes*
Total Time: *25 minutes*
Makes *a first course for 6*

I've tried to make just about every version of fried rice that exists. Pineapple fried rice, kimchi fried rice, and shrimp fried rice. Can you tell I was obsessed? Crab fried rice, by far, is the easiest one to execute. Whenever I wonder what to do with the day-old rice in my fridge, I think, "crab fried rice!" Chilled medium-grain white rice works best because the drier grains make it perfect for stir-frying. It also holds its shape better under the weight of the moisture. And if you try making fried rice with a fresh pot of rice, it'll be soooo clumpy. The crab's salty fish flavor should be at the forefront of this dish, so make sure you use quality lump crab and avoid imitation crab. I've also been known to finish the plate with an additional crispy fried egg on top. If you have the time to do it, you'll thank me later!

3 tablespoons **vegetable oil**

6 **garlic cloves**, chopped

2 cups **day-old cooked rice**

1 cup **lump crabmeat**

1 tablespoon **soy sauce**

2 teaspoons **fish sauce**

1 teaspoon **sugar**

2 **large eggs**

2 **scallions**, thinly sliced

2 tablespoons (packed) **fresh cilantro leaves** (stems removed)

1   Heat the vegetable oil in a large sauté pan over medium heat until it is shimmering, about 2 minutes. Add the garlic and cook, stirring, until it turns golden, 1 to 2 minutes.

2   Increase the heat to high. Add the rice, crabmeat, soy sauce, fish sauce, and sugar. Toss it all together with a spatula and make sure to break up any clumps of rice.

3   In a small bowl, whisk the eggs. Scoot the rice to the side of the pan with a spatula and pour the eggs into the empty side. Scramble the eggs slightly with the whisk. Let the eggs cook until set and no longer runny, 1 to 2 minutes. Break it up with a spatula, then toss the egg into the rice.

4   Use the back of a spatula to flatten the rice and fry it undisturbed for 30 seconds. Toss it again to break up the crisped-up bits. Repeat this step three more times.

5   Transfer the rice to a plate and garnish with the scallions and cilantro.

CLASSICS

Pork & Vermicelli Bowl

Bún Chả

Prep Time: *1 hour 20 minutes*
Total Time: *2 hours 20 minutes*
Makes *a main course for 4*

Bún chà hails from North Vietnam, where the cuisine is much more understated and subtle compared to the boldness and spice of its southern counterpart. I've never been up north, but my cousin's uncle lived there and treated us to bún chà when he came to visit. It's fresh, savory, sweet, and herby all at the same time. Traditional bún chà features rice vermicelli noodles served with a vegetal broth, seasoned pork patties, and caramelized pork belly slices. My version presents you with several dining options. You can either dip the noodles in the sauce mixture, pour the sauce all over the noodles, or enjoy it as a lettuce wrap. When you choose the lettuce to use, you can use anything but iceberg—it's too watery! I recommend seeking out Persian (mini) cucumbers because they're seedless and add an extra crispy texture to the experience. The pork patties are best when they're grilled, but if you don't have easy access to a grill, you can pan-sear them instead.

PORK PATTIES:

1 pound **ground pork**

¼ **white onion,** minced

4 **garlic cloves,** minced

1 tablespoon **fish sauce**

1 tablespoon **soy sauce**

1 tablespoon **sugar**

1 tablespoon **vegetable oil**

SAUCE:

½ cup **fish sauce**

½ cup **sugar**

2 tablespoons **distilled white vinegar**

1 **lime,** cut into wedges

FOR SERVING:

14 ounces **rice vermicelli noodles**

1 head **lettuce,** roughly chopped

2 **scallions,** thinly sliced

1 cup (packed) **fresh mint** or **cilantro leaves,** roughly chopped

1 **Persian** (mini) **cucumber,** thinly sliced

1 **lime,** cut into wedges

1 **carrot,** peeled and cut into thin coins or flower shapes

¼ cup **chopped peanuts**

1   Make the pork patties: In a large bowl, combine the ground pork, onion, garlic, fish sauce, soy sauce, and sugar. Mix thoroughly. Cover with plastic wrap and refrigerate for 30 minutes to 1 hour.

2   Form the chilled meat mixture into 8 burger-like patties, weighing around 2 ounces each. Brush the vegetable oil over the patties.

3   If you're using a grill: Preheat the grill to high. Grill the patties 4 to 6 minutes per side, until charred and cooked to an internal temperature of 165°F. Transfer the patties to a plate to rest.

4   If you don't have a grill: Preheat a 12-inch skillet over medium heat for 2 to 3 minutes. Add the patties to the pan oil-side down and brush the other sides. Fry until browned on the bottom, 2 to 3 minutes. Flip them over and brown the other sides until cooked through to an internal temperature of 165°F, another 2 to 3 minutes.

5   Make the sauce: In a small bowl, whisk together the fish sauce, ½ cup water, the sugar, vinegar, and juice of 2 or 3 lime wedges. Taste and adjust to your liking with more lime juice, if needed.

6   To serve: Cook the vermicelli noodles according to the package directions.

7   On a serving platter, lay down a bed of the lettuce, scallions, and fresh mint. Pile on the vermicelli, cucumber, and pork patties. Serve with the sauce in a small bowl on the side with more lime wedges.

8   Nestle a few carrot pieces between the noodles and sprinkle some peanuts over each bowl.

Vietnamese Crepes

Bánh Xèo

Prep Time: *1 hour 20 minutes*
Total Time: *2 hours*
Makes *10 to 12 crepes*

Bánh xèo is a crispy Vietnamese crepe and happens to be my mom's favorite dish. At first glance, most people mistake it for a giant omelet. The recipe is seemingly simple but takes some finesse to get it right. On my first attempt to make bánh xèo myself, the batter either burned, stuck to the pan, or just wasn't crispy enough. I went through so much trial and error. I tried all kinds of pans and cooking methods to get this right. Trust me when I say this: The key to a light and crispy bánh xèo is a nonstick pan and a lot of oil. You can use whatever oil you prefer, but it's important to note that it's not primarily for sautéing but for releasing the crepe from the pan. Don't be discouraged if the cooking method is tricky; it might take some practice, but you can definitely get it after one or two tries.

Once you master bánh xèo, it can be customized almost entirely! If you're not able to find any coconut soda, no biggie, you can substitute it with water.

(recipe continues)

1 (13.5-ounce) **can coconut milk**

½ cup **rice flour**

½ cup **coconut soda**

1 teaspoon **ground turmeric**

4 **scallions**, chopped

2 tablespoons **vegetable oil**, plus more for frying

½ pound **skinless pork belly**, thinly sliced

½ pound **shrimp**, peeled and deveined

½ **white onion**, thinly sliced

½ pound **mung bean sprouts**, for serving

1 **Persian** (mini) **cucumber**, sliced thinly

½ head **red lettuce**, separated into leaves

¼ packed cup **fresh mint**

½ cup **Nước Mắm** (page 173), for serving

1. In a large bowl, combine the coconut milk, rice flour, coconut soda, turmeric, and scallions. Give it a good whisk and place it in the fridge so the flour can bloom, for at least 30 minutes and up to 1 hour.

2. Set a 12-inch nonstick skillet over high heat for 1 minute. Dip a folded-up paper towel in the vegetable oil, and use tongs to lightly wipe it around the inside of the skillet. When the skillet is nice and hot, add 2 or 3 pieces of the pork belly, 1 shrimp, and a few onion slices to the skillet. Cook, stirring, until the pork belly and shrimp have turned opaque, about 1 minute. Spread the protein and onion pieces evenly across the pan.

3. Pour ½ cup of the rice flour batter over the proteins and spread it evenly by carefully tilting the skillet around. Cover the skillet with a lid for 1 minute 30 seconds. Uncover and reduce the heat to medium-low. Brush vegetable oil on the outer edges of the bánh xèo. Cover again and cook until the edges curl away from the skillet and the batter does not look wet, another 1 minute 30 seconds. Using a spatula, fold the crepe in half and transfer it to a plate.

4. Repeat the process until you're out of batter. If the crepes burn, turn your heat down slightly when you cook the proteins and carefully wipe the skillet with the oil-soaked paper towel before making another one.

5. Enjoy bánh xèo with a side of bean sprouts, cucumber slices, red lettuce, fresh mint, and nước mắm in a small bowl in a small bowl.

Grilled Pork Chops
Broken Rice Plate

Cơm
Tấm

Prep Time: *1 hour 10 minutes*
Total Time: *3 hours 25 minutes*
Makes *a complete meal for 4*

In Vietnam, street vendors grill pork chops over charcoal grills and the aroma draws crowds of people to come eat. I have fond memories of eating broken rice plates before going to school. Broken rice refers to the grains that get damaged during the milling process. These fractured, smaller grains are able to hold flavors and absorb liquid easily—making them perfect for soaking up the pan juices from pork chops. Typically, this dish is meant to be eaten for breakfast, but if it feels too heavy to you, don't worry because it hits just the same at any other point of the day. While it's an extra step, do yourself a favor and make the Scallion Oil (page 177), it really completes the meal.

$\frac{1}{4}$ cup **minced shallots**

$\frac{1}{4}$ cup **fish sauce**

2 tablespoons **minced garlic**

2 tablespoons **minced fresh lemongrass**

2 tablespoons **soy sauce**

2 tablespoons **honey**

1 tablespoon **light brown sugar**

4 **bone-in pork chops** (8 ounces each), $\frac{1}{2}$ inch thick

2 cups **broken jasmine rice**

2 tablespoons **vegetable oil**

4 **large eggs**

2 **Persian** (mini) **cucumbers**, peeled and thinly sliced

$\frac{1}{4}$ cup **Đồ Chua** (page 191)

$\frac{1}{4}$ cup **Scallion Oil** (optional; page 177)

$\frac{3}{4}$ cup **Nước Mắm** (page 173)

1   In a large bowl or deep baking dish, whisk together the shallots, fish sauce, garlic, lemongrass, soy sauce, honey, and brown sugar. Place the pork chops in the marinade and turn to coat thoroughly. Cover with plastic wrap and marinate for at least 1 hour at room temperature or in the fridge overnight.

2   Rinse the broken rice with cold water until the water runs clear. Drain it thoroughly.

3   If using a rice cooker: In the bowl of a rice cooker, combine the washed rice with $2\frac{1}{4}$ cups water. Turn on the cooker or choose the white rice setting, which may take 20 to 30 minutes.

(recipe continues)

4   If cooking rice on the stovetop: In a saucepan, combine the rice and 2¼ cups water. Bring it to a boil over medium-high heat, uncovered. Once boiling, reduce the heat to medium-low, cover, and steam for 12 minutes. Remove from the heat and let stand for 10 minutes.

5   Preheat the oven to 375°F.

6   Arrange the pork chops in a single layer on a sheet pan and roast for 20 minutes. Remove the pork chops from the oven.

7   Preheat a cast-iron skillet over medium-high heat. Once it is smoking, sear the pork chops until they are charred on the edges, about 2 minutes on each side. Remove them to a plate and let rest.

8   Line a plate with paper towels. In the same skillet, heat the vegetable oil. Crack in the eggs, one at a time, and cook them sunny-side up, or until the whites are set and no longer runny, 3 to 5 minutes. To get crispy edges, use a spoon to carefully baste the whites of the egg with the hot oil. Transfer the fried egg to the paper towel lined plate to drain. Repeat frying with the remaining eggs.

9   Divide the rice among four plates. For each plate, add a pork chop, a fried egg, a few pieces of sliced cucumber, and 1 tablespoon đồ chua. Drizzle a little scallion oil (if using) over the pork chop and rice. Serve the nước mắm on the side in a small bowl.

Crispy Pork Belly

Prep Time: *1 hour*

Total Time: *2 hours 30 minutes*

Makes *a first course for 4 or main course for 2*

Pork belly is one of my favorite meats to use because it is succulent, flavorful, and can play so many different roles in the food world from bacon to lechon. Pork belly also stars in my Thịt Kho (page 42), Nem Nướng (page 96), and Bánh Xèo (page 50). I'll admit, crispy pork belly can be time-consuming. I've done my best to shorten the length of time it takes to make it so you can get to impress your friends and family quicker. The vinegar brushing step seems tedious, but bear with me! It'll help crisp it up and crown the pork belly skin with a tangy kick. Pro tip: The longer you dry the pork belly in the fridge, the crispier the skin will be. I know it's always so tough to wait, but your first crunchy bite will make you glad you were patient.

1 pound **skin-on pork belly**

2 teaspoons **sugar**

1½ teaspoons **five-spice powder**

1½ teaspoons **garlic powder**

1 teaspoon **soy sauce**

1 teaspoon **oyster sauce**

2 tablespoons **distilled white vinegar**

3 tablespoons **kosher salt**

1   Pat the pork belly dry with paper towels. Use a fork to poke holes into the skin. Make sure that every inch of the skin is covered with holes; it's around 50 to 60 stabs. Pat the skin dry again and turn the pork belly over to the meat side and score it with a sharp knife in a crosshatch pattern (don't cut all the way through it!).

2   In a small bowl, mix together the sugar, five-spice powder, garlic powder, soy sauce, and oyster sauce. Spread the spice mixture on the meat side, making sure to get into the crevices, too. Wrap a sheet of foil around the bottom and sides of the pork belly, leaving the skin exposed. Place it on a sheet pan and refrigerate uncovered for 1 hour or up to overnight, the longer the better.

3   Once you run out of patience waiting for the pork to marinate and dry out, position a rack in the middle of the oven and preheat the oven to 350°F.

4   Remove the pork belly from the fridge. Brush a few layers of vinegar on the skin side of the pork belly and coat it in salt, but don't worry! The pork belly won't be salty.

5   When the oven is up to temperature, take the foil off and place the pork belly on a wire rack nested in a sheet pan. Roast the pork until the salt dries out and hardens, about 20 minutes. Take it out of the oven and increase the oven temperature to 450°F.

6   Carefully brush off the salt layer with a spatula. Poke more holes in the skin with a fork and brush the skin side of the pork belly again with more vinegar. Using tongs, flip the pork belly skin-side down and roast in the oven until the marinated meat has browned, 10 to 15 minutes. If not, continue to cook for up to another 15 minutes, checking every 5 minutes.

7   Take it out and flip it skin-side up again. Brush a final layer of vinegar on the skin. Roast until the meat side is uniformly browned and the internal temperature has reached 165°F, another 15 to 20 minutes.

8   Remove the pork from the oven. Switch the oven to broil and cook the pork belly skin-side up on the top rack, watching the skin of the pork belly bubble and crisp, up to 5 minutes, keeping an eye out for any burning.

9   Carefully transfer the pork belly to a cutting board. Slice it up into ½-inch bite-size pieces and transfer to a plate.

Chả Giò, page 60

Rice Paper Egg Rolls

Chả Giò

Prep Time: *25 minutes*

Total Time: *1 hour 40 minutes*

Makes *40 egg rolls*

Egg rolls are ubiquitous in Asian cuisine, whether it's Chinese, Filipino, Thai, or Vietnamese. The most popular types are made with a wheat flour–based wrapper. However, the Vietnamese version really stands out because we use rice paper instead. The result is a crispy bite that has a bit of a chewy texture to it, which is so addictive to eat. This recipe uses shrimp and ground pork in the filling, but you can switch up the protein with ground turkey, chicken, or beef if you're feeling bold! These egg rolls are a surefire crowd-pleaser, I'd recommend making some for Friendsgiving or a Lunar New Year party.

- 3 heaping tablespoons **dried wood ear mushrooms**
- **Hot water,** for soaking
- 2 ounces **mung bean cellophane noodles** (aka **bean thread**)

- ½ pound **ground pork**
- ½ pound medium **shrimp,** peeled, deveined, and minced
- ¾ cup shredded peeled **carrot**
- 1 small **shallot,** minced

- 1 **large egg**
- 2 tablespoons **fish sauce**
- 3 teaspoons **granulated sugar**
- 1 tablespoon **distilled white vinegar**
- 40 **rice paper rounds**

- **Vegetable oil** for deep-frying (about 1 quart)
- ½ cup **Sweet Chili Sauce** (page 185), for serving
- ½ cup **Peanut Sauce** (page 179), for serving

1   In a heatproof bowl, combine the wood ear mushrooms and enough hot water to cover and let soak for 10 minutes. When they're cool enough to handle, rub lightly to remove any grit, and drain off the water.

2   In another heatproof bowl, combine the cellophane noodles and enough hot water to cover them and soak until softened, about 2 minutes. Drain the noodles.

3   Roughly chop the noodles and wood ear mushrooms together. Pat dry with a paper towel.

4   In a separate bowl, combine the ground pork, shrimp, carrots, shallot, egg, and the mushroom mixture. Season it with the fish sauce and 2 teaspoons of the sugar. Mix it well.

5   Fill a wide, shallow bowl with warm water. Add the remaining 1 teaspoon sugar and the vinegar and whisk until the sugar dissolves.

6   Soak a round of rice paper in the warm water mixture until it is pliable, 2 or 3 seconds. Lay it flat on a clean, dry surface. Lightly pat it dry with a paper towel. Scoop 1 heaping tablespoon of meat mixture into the center.

7   Wrap up the egg roll the way you would wrap a burrito: Bring the bottom flap tightly over the filling and roll it forward slightly to spread the filling into a 3-inch-wide tube. Fold the left and right flaps toward the center so they overlap evenly over the filling. Roll the tube forward to close it. Set aside on a plate. Repeat with the remaining rice paper rounds and filling.

8   Pour 3 inches of vegetable oil into a 4-quart deep, heavy pot or a deep fryer and heat over medium-high heat to 350°F. Use a wooden chopstick to test the oil if it is hot enough, it should bubble actively. Nest a wire rack in a sheet pan and set it near the stove. Working in batches of 10 to 12, fry the egg rolls until they float and go from opaque white to a bubbly translucence, about 5 minutes. Check periodically as they fry to see if they stick together and carefully separate them with tongs. Remove from the oil and drain on the wire rack.

9   Transfer the rolls to a serving platter. Serve with the sweet chili sauce and peanut sauce in small bowls for dipping.

Clear Dumplings

Bánh Bột Lọc

Prep Time: *40 minutes*

Total Time: *2 hours 40 minutes*

Makes *40 dumplings*

I know I shouldn't play favorites, guys, but I have to confess that bánh bột lọc is my all-time favorite Vietnamese street snack. I can't resist its chewy texture, savory filling, and literal bath of fish sauce. The dumpling dough is made of tapioca starch, which is what gives it a translucent finish and a bite similar to mochi. When I immigrated to the United States, it was almost impossible to find any places that sold bánh bột lọc. The versions I found were not what I was used to: wrapped in banana leaves and not swimming in fish sauce. It was my mission to share the recipe for the version of this dish that I've grown up with. I looked to the Internet for help and found a tutorial on YouTube (which people online call YouTube University). I practiced it a bunch of times until I got it right. You can choose to use leaner pork if you'd like, but I highly recommend this recipe as it is!

Canola oil

½ pound **skinless pork belly,** diced

3 tablespoons **minced shallots**

½ pound **shrimp,** peeled, deveined, and minced

½ tablespoon **fish sauce,** plus more for serving

2 teaspoons **sugar**

3 cups **tapioca starch** (aka **tapioca flour**)

1½ cups **boiling water**

¼ cup **Scallion Oil** (page 177)

¼ cup **Nước Mắm** (page 173), plus more to taste

¼ cup **Fried Shallots** (page 194)

1 Add 2 tablespoons canola oil (or enough to coat the bottom) to a small 8-inch skillet and heat over medium-high heat for 1 minute. Add the diced pork belly and cook, stirring until browned on the edges, about 5 minutes. Add the shallots and cook, stirring occasionally, until the shallots are translucent, 2 to 3 minutes.

2 Add the shrimp, toss once, then add the fish sauce and sugar. Cook until the shrimp is fully pink, 2 to 3 minutes longer. Remove from the heat and let the filling cool in the pan.

3 In a large bowl, stir together the tapioca starch and boiling water. Mix the dough with a spatula until it is cool enough to handle. Using clean hands, work and knead the dough in the bowl until it becomes cohesive, tacky, and gummy. Let it cool completely and uncovered, 10 to 15 minutes.

4 Bring a pot of water to a boil over high heat, then reduce it to a simmer over medium-low heat. Set up a large bowl of ice and water and have it near the stove.

5 Form the dough into 1-inch balls. With a rolling pin, flatten each ball into a thin round $2\frac{1}{2}$ to 3 inches across. Place 1 teaspoon of filling in the center of each, fold the rounds into a half-moon shape, and press the edges closed. Once you've finished making the dumplings, place half of them into the pot of boiling water.

6 Once the dumplings start to float, cook for an additional 2 to 3 minutes to activate the tapioca starch.

7 Shock the finished dumplings in the ice bath and watch the magic happen! They will instantly turn into clear dumplings. Once they are cooled, scoop the dumplings out of the ice bath and place on a platter. Repeat the process with the other half of the dumplings

8 Drizzle the scallion oil and nước mắm over the dumplings. Finish with a scattering of fried shallots.

Do you ever look back on your life and think, "Tha[...]

colossal role in who I am today and how I got here[...]

alter the trajectory of your entire life. Going vira[...]

also helped shape my cooking style and defined who[...]

and values, I discovered two vital truths. First, I[...]

show people that cooking doesn't have to be scary c[...]

as delicious as anything abstract or[...]

amount of interest online,[...]

Internet

moment changed my life"? The following recipes played a

They're evidence that little moments can dramatically

with recipes not only catapulted my career, but it

am as a chef. While I explored my Vietnamese identity

want to demystify Vietnamese cooking. Second, I want to

ntimidating. Food can be straight to the point and just

ontemporary. While these dishes garnered a significant

you'll find the recipes in this chapter are tried and

true, a collection that you can always revisit when

you're looking for something new.

F a m o u s

Lemongrass Chicken

Prep Time: *1 hour 40 minutes*

Total Time: *2 hours 25 minutes*

Makes *a first course for 4 or a main course for 2*

Lemongrass chicken is the first Vietnamese recipe I learned how to make when I moved out of my parents' house in 2016 to go to culinary school. Before that point, I would split a plate from Panda Express for breakfast, lunch, and dinner. I was really missing the smells and tastes of home! Nothing made me more homesick than the scent of lemongrass. I enjoy using boneless chicken thighs for this, but you can also use shrimp, pork, or tofu as well.

4 **boneless, skin-on chicken thighs**

2 tablespoons **minced garlic**

2 tablespoons **minced fresh lemongrass**

2 tablespoons **fish sauce**

2 tablespoons **sugar**

2 to 3 **fresh Thai bird's eye chilies**, to taste, thinly sliced

$\frac{1}{2}$ cup **vegetable oil**

1 **scallion**, julienned

Steamed White Rice (page 26), for serving

1   Cut the chicken thighs into 1-inch pieces and place in a large bowl. Add the garlic, lemongrass, fish sauce, sugar, and chilies. Massage the chicken to thoroughly combine with the marinade. Cover and refrigerate for 30 minutes to 1 hour, or better yet, overnight! The more you let it marinate, the more flavor it will develop.

2   Heat $\frac{1}{4}$ cup of the vegetable oil in a 10-inch sauté pan over medium-high heat until it is shimmering, 2 to 3 minutes. Add half of the chicken pieces in a single layer and cook to get a nice deep brown color, 6 to 8 minutes. Flip the pieces and continue cooking until all the pieces are a little browned, fully opaque, and no longer pink, about 6 minutes longer. Transfer the cooked chicken to a plate. Add the remaining $\frac{1}{4}$ cup vegetable oil to the pan and repeat with the remaining chicken.

3   Serve the chicken in a bowl over freshly steamed white rice.

This recipe holds a special place in my heart because it was the first dish that I ever came up with in culinary school. In a way, it gave me the confidence to start developing my own recipes. During my garde manger class, we were tasked with coming up with our own recipe for finger foods. I paired it with an avocado mousse and a crispy wonton chip. Everyone in class loved it, so I knew I had the beginnings of something great. I decided to share the simplified shrimp recipe with the Internet and it was a hit! It is a super-simple, incredibly delicious, and versatile dish because you can use any protein with this glaze. I've used pork butt, chicken thigh, and filet mignon in the past as a substitute for shrimp.

Honey-Glazed Shrimp

Prep Time: *10 minutes*

Total Time: *35 minutes*

Makes *a first course for 4 or a main course for 2*

½ pound **jumbo shrimp**, peeled and deveined (leave the tails attached)

1 **large egg white**

½ cup **cornstarch**

½ teaspoon **kosher salt**

½ teaspoon **freshly ground black pepper**

1 cup **avocado oil**

3 tablespoons **honey**

2 tablespoons **soy sauce**

2 tablespoons **apple cider vinegar**

1 tablespoon **oyster sauce**

1 teaspoon **cayenne pepper**

1½ teaspoons **red pepper flakes**

1 **scallion**, julienned

Steamed White Rice (page 26), for serving

1   Pat the shrimp dry with a paper towel and set aside.

2   In a small bowl, whisk the egg white until it gets nice and foamy. In another small bowl, stir together the cornstarch, salt, and black pepper.

3   Nest a wire rack in a sheet pan. Dip the shrimp into the egg white foam and dunk into the cornstarch. Make sure that they are nice and coated on both sides. Tap off any excess starch. Place them on the prepared sheet pan as you work.

(recipe continues)

4   Line a plate with paper towels and keep it near the stove. Heat the avocado oil in an 8-inch sauté pan over high heat until shimmering, 2 to 3 minutes. Place the coated shrimp in the pan and shallow-fry until it develops a golden-brown crust, about 30 seconds. Flip the shrimp and cook for another 30 seconds so the other side develops color. Transfer the shrimp to the paper towels to drain.

5   In a small bowl, combine the honey, soy sauce, vinegar, oyster sauce, cayenne, and pepper flakes. Mix well with a spoon.

6   Pour off all but about 1 tablespoon of avocado oil (or enough to coat the bottom) from the sauté pan. Save the excess oil for another use. Reduce the heat to medium and carefully pour the glaze mixture into the pan. Stir until the sauce thickens, 3 to 4 minutes. Add the cooked shrimp to the sauce and toss so that every piece is coated.

7   Transfer the glazed shrimp to a serving plate and garnish with the scallion. Enjoy with steamed white rice.

I was at a family party in Oxnard, California, and I took a bite of the best wings I have ever had in my life. In my life! I asked the cook, a family friend, for her recipe, but she would not give it up. From that moment, it became my life's mission to re-create it. It was a journey, because it can be tricky to balance the high saltiness of fish sauce with sweet flavors. It took a lot of tries, but I've been serving these wings at almost all my pop-ups for hundreds of guests at a time. I opt for full chicken wings, with the wing tip, flat, and drumette still connected. It's easy to scale up the recipe for a party, too. The marinade will always be equal parts fish sauce to sugar. Fish sauce wings have consistently been a hit and I'm confident you'll love them.

Fish Sauce Wings

Cánh Gà Chiên Nước Mắm

Prep Time: *2 hours 20 minutes*

Total Time: *2 hours 50 minutes*

Makes *a first course for 4 or a main course for 2*

1 cup **fish sauce**

1 cup **sugar**

3 pounds **chicken wings**

12 **garlic cloves,** smashed and peeled

Canola oil for deep-frying (about 2 quarts)

¾ cup **potato starch**

2 **scallions,** thinly sliced on a diagonal

1 tablespoon **Fried Shallots** (page 194)

¼ cup **Bomb-Ass Ranch** (page 178)

¼ cup **Sweet Chili Sauce** (page 185)

1   In a small bowl, whisk together the fish sauce and sugar until the sugar dissolves. Place the chicken wings and garlic in a plastic zipper bag or large bowl and pour the fish sauce marinade over the chicken. Massage or toss the chicken to make sure every piece is coated. Seal the bag or cover the bowl with plastic wrap and

(recipe continues)

marinate in the fridge for at least 2 hours, but I recommend doing it overnight!

2   Pour 4 inches of canola oil into a Dutch oven or a deep fryer and heat over medium heat to 300°F.

3   Nest a wire rack in a sheet pan. Add the potato starch to a shallow bowl or sheet pan. Drain the marinade from the wings and discard the garlic. Coat the wings thoroughly on both sides in the potato starch, tap off any excess, and set on the prepared wire rack.

4   Working in batches, carefully add a single layer of wings to the hot oil and cook until the chicken flesh turns opaque and the starch no

longer looks dry and powdery, 5 to 6 minutes. Use tongs to return the wings to the wire rack. Bring the oil back up to temperature between batches.

5   Increase the oil temperature to 350°F.

6   Place a clean wire rack in the sheet pan and set near the stove. Again, working in batches, carefully return the wings to the hot oil in a single layer until the skin crisps up and toasts to a nice brown, 4 to 5 minutes. Drain the wings on the clean wire rack. Bring the oil back up to temperature between batches.

7   Transfer the wings to a platter and garnish with the scallions and fried shallots. Serve the ranch and sweet chili sauce in small bowls on the side.

Pork Meatballs

Xíu Mại

Prep Time: *25 minutes*

Total Time: *1 hour 25 minutes*

Makes *a first course for 4 or a main course for 2*

I grew up in a beach town near the southern end of Vietnam. Vũng Tàu is a beautiful, picturesque coastal city that attracts both tourists and locals. I remember spending a lot of time playing in the warm waters of the beach with my dad because it was so close to our house. After our day in the sun was done, he would take me to get bánh mì xíu mại to restore all the energy we exhausted. I have such fond, sentimental memories of biting into crisp airy bread and savory meatballs with a burst of tomato umami. Every time I have xíu mại, it brings me right back to that little beach town and I can't help but feel nostalgic joy.

You have free rein to play around with the meatball sizes as you see fit. Make them as big or as small as you'd like; they work as either an appetizer or a main course. Do not cook the meatballs all the way through: You're only looking for a nice sear on them because they will finish cooking in the sauce.

8 **Roma (plum) tomatoes,** cored and quartered

¼ teaspoon **kosher salt**

1 pound **ground pork**

2 **scallions,** minced

½ cup **minced peeled jicama**

1 **shallot,** minced

Cloves from 1 head **garlic,** minced

3 tablespoons **sugar**

3 tablespoons **panko bread crumbs**

2 tablespoons **oyster sauce**

2 tablespoons **fish sauce,** plus more to taste

1 tablespoon **soy sauce**

1 **large egg**

2 tablespoons **vegetable oil**

1 **lime,** cut into wedges

½ cup (packed) **fresh cilantro leaves** (stems removed)

¼ teaspoon **freshly ground black pepper**

Baguette or **Steamed White Rice** (page 26), for serving

1. Preheat the oven to 400°F.

2. Lightly salt the tomato pieces on a baking sheet. Roast until the skin starts to blister and release juice, 10 to 15 minutes. Remove from the oven and set aside to cool.

3. In a large bowl, combine the ground pork, scallions, jicama, half the shallot, and half the garlic. With clean hands, mix the meat mixture. Add the sugar, panko, oyster sauce, fish sauce, soy sauce, and egg and gently combine. Form the meat mixture into 8 meatballs.

4. Preheat a skillet over medium-high heat for 1 minute. Add the meatballs and sear until browned, about 1 minute. Flip and sear the other sides for another minute. Remove from the pan and set aside on a plate.

5. Add the vegetable oil and the remaining shallot and garlic to the pan and cook, stirring until the garlic turns golden (not golden brown, just golden!), 1 to 2 minutes. Add the roasted tomatoes with their skin and juice and mash it all together with a wooden spoon.

6. Reduce the heat to medium and cook until the tomatoes become saucy, stirring occasionally, 5 to 8 minutes.

7. Adjust the seasoning with fish sauce and a squeeze of lime juice if needed. Return the meatballs to the pan. Cover and cook over medium-low heat until the meatballs are no longer pink on the inside or reach an internal temperature of 165°F, 10 to 15 minutes.

8. Garnish with the cilantro and black pepper. Serve the meatballs on a sliced baguette or over a bowl of steamed white rice with lime wedges on the side.

Viral Fried Rice, page 76

Viral Fried Rice

Prep Time: *15 minutes*
Total Time: *40 minutes*
Makes *a first course for 4*

If you've been following me since day one, you know how important and life-changing this fried rice was for me. Can you believe fried rice completely altered the trajectory of my life and led me to writing this cookbook you're holding in your hands? What makes this recipe unique are the final steps of crisping up the rice. I accomplish this with a flat-bottomed wok from Frök (read more on page 19), but if you don't have that, a wok or large sauté pan works just as well.

I highly recommend using day-old rice, because fresh rice tends to form clumps when it is fried. You want the grains to be dried out and firm enough to fry over high heat. Chinese lap cheong sausages are my preferred protein because they're cured with sugar, soy sauce, and then smoked—resulting in a saltier, sweeter, and smokier bite than regular pork sausages.

5 tablespoons **sriracha**

5 tablespoons **soy sauce**

2 **large eggs**

2 teaspoons **fish sauce**

2 **lap cheong Chinese sausages**, halved lengthwise and thinly sliced crosswise into half-moons

1 **carrot**, peeled and finely diced

4 **garlic cloves**, minced

½ **yellow onion**, diced

2 cups **Steamed White Rice** (page 26), chilled

3 **scallions**, thinly sliced

Freshly ground black pepper

1   In a small bowl, stir the sriracha and soy sauce together. In another small bowl, scramble the eggs and fish sauce with a fork. Set aside.

2   Cook the Chinese sausage in a flat-bottomed wok or regular wok over medium-high heat until the fat renders, about 2 minutes. Add the carrot, garlic, and yellow onion to the pan and cook, stirring occasionally, until the onion softens, 2 to 3 minutes.

3   Crumble the cooked rice into the pan and toss it around once with a spatula. Pour the sriracha mixture over the rice. Mix it until all the grains of rice are coated.

4   Scoot the rice to the side of the pan leaving an empty space for the eggs. Add the eggs to the pan and let them firm up for 2 to 3 minutes before breaking them up and mixing into the rice.

5   After everything is mixed, reduce the heat to medium and flatten the rice out by pressing it down into the pan with a spatula. Cook undisturbed so the rice can crisp up, 1 to 2 minutes. Break it up and repeat this step two more times.

6   Transfer the fried rice to a platter. Garnish with the scallions and a few pinches of black pepper.

Garlic Noodles

Prep Time: *15 minutes*

Total Time: *40 minutes*

Makes *a first course for 4 or a main course for 2*

Big thumbs up to the first person in history who decided to combine garlic and noodles in a dish, because whenever I see them on a menu, I order them. I feel like they can never steer you wrong. I didn't realize how easy it was to make at home until I tried it myself. My version was a hit online because 1) It's delicious (duh) and 2) It's a surefire and simple meal to make. I serve my garlic noodles with shrimp, but you can substitute grilled chicken or lump crab if that's more your style. This one goes out to my garlic girlies out there!

$\frac{1}{4}$ cup plus $\frac{1}{2}$ teaspoon **kosher salt**

8 ounces **angel hair pasta**

$\frac{1}{2}$ pound **jumbo shrimp**, peeled

$\frac{1}{2}$ teaspoon **freshly ground black pepper**, plus more to taste

2 teaspoons plus a pinch **red pepper flakes** (optional)

5 tablespoons **unsalted butter**

10 **garlic cloves**, finely chopped

$\frac{1}{2}$ teaspoon **garlic salt**

2 tablespoons **soy sauce**

2 tablespoons **oyster sauce**

2 teaspoons **fish sauce** (optional)

Freshly grated **Parmesan cheese**, for serving

2 **scallions**, thinly sliced on the diagonal

1   In a large pot, bring 2 quarts water and $\frac{1}{4}$ cup of the kosher salt to a boil. Add the angel hair pasta and cook according to the package directions. Reserving 1 cup of the pasta water, drain the pasta.

2   In a small bowl, toss the shrimp with the remaining $\frac{1}{2}$ teaspoon salt, the black pepper, and 2 teaspoons pepper flakes (if using).

3   Heat a large sauté pan over high heat for 1 minute. Add 1 tablespoon of the butter and let it melt. Sear the shrimp on each side until they turn pink, about 1 minute. Remove the seared shrimp to a plate.

4   Set the pan over medium heat, add the butter to melt, then stir in the garlic and garlic salt. Once incorporated, add the soy sauce, oyster sauce, fish sauce (if using), and another pinch of pepper flakes (if using). Cook until it starts to bubble, about 1 minute. Using tongs, fold in the cooked pasta until completely coated with the sauce. Add the shrimp and toss again until combined.

5   Increase the heat under the pan to medium-high and toss for an additional 1 to 2 minutes.

Most of the liquid should be absorbed but the pan should not be totally dry. If it's too dry, add some of the reserved pasta water 1 to 2 tablespoons at a time until you get it to a saucy consistency.

6   Adjust the seasoning to taste with salt, pepper, and fish sauce (if using). Transfer the pasta to a large bowl. Garnish with some Parmesan and the scallions.

Lemongrass Chili Oil Noodles

Prep Time: *5 minutes*

Total Time: *30 minutes*

Makes *a first course for 4 or main course for 2*

CHILI OIL SAUCE:

3 tablespoons **Lemongrass Chili Oil** (page 186)

2 tablespoons **Chinkiang black vinegar**

1 tablespoon **soy sauce**

1 teaspoon **sesame paste**

NOODLES AND BEEF:

8 ounces **Taiwanese squiggly noodles** or **wheat-based noodles** (about 2 packs)

½ pound **ground beef** (80/20)

Cloves from 1 head **garlic**, minced

½ teaspoon **kosher salt**

½ teaspoon **freshly ground black pepper**

1 tablespoon **soy sauce**

1 tablespoon **Chinkiang black vinegar**

6 **fresh Thai basil** or **basil leaves**

FOR SERVING:

¼ teaspoon **sesame oil** (optional)

2 **scallions**, thinly sliced

1 teaspoon **sesame seeds**, toasted

For a time, I was obsessed with making chili oil noodles because I saw them on Instagram. With each bowl, I couldn't shake the feeling that adding lemongrass would make them even more delicious. Spoiler alert! I was right. To round out the flavor, I recommend using sesame paste, but you can substitute with tahini if you can't get your hands on any. The key to this dish is to not oil the pan. The ground beef has a ton of its own natural fat, and I drain it off after the meat browns, because the excess fat makes it harder for the chili oil to grip onto the noodles.

1   Make the chili oil sauce: In a small bowl, whisk together the lemongrass chili oil, black vinegar, soy sauce, and sesame paste until combined. Set aside.

2   Cook the noodles and beef: Cook the noodles according to the package directions. Drain and set aside.

3   Preheat a large sauté pan over medium-high heat for 1 minute. Add the ground beef and garlic and cook, stirring, until the beef turns from red to light brown, 3 to 4 minutes. Do your best to break up the ground meat with a wooden spoon. Season the beef with the salt and pepper and give it a good mix.

4 Drain off the excess "beef juice" by putting the beef into a fine-mesh sieve. Alternatively, you can scoot the meat to one side and tilt the pan to spoon out excess drippings.

5 Return the meat to the pan and set over medium-high heat. Stir in the soy sauce, black vinegar, and basil leaves and cook until the beef is no longer pink and is completely browned, 3 to 4 minutes. Remove from the heat.

6 To serve: Spoon the chili oil sauce into a large bowl or a deep dish, layer on the cooked noodles, scoop the ground beef over the noodles, drizzle with the sesame oil (if using), top with the scallions, and sprinkle with the toasted sesame seeds. Toss together and enjoy hot.

Seafood Boil Pasta

Prep Time: *40 minutes*

Total Time: *1 hour*

Makes *a first course for 4 or main course for 2*

I was eating a bountiful seafood boil one day and the idea came to me, "You know, this would be great if I had noodles to soak up all of this sauce." A lot of people feel very strongly against angel hair, but it's my preferred pasta shape. I enjoy the texture and it's easier for this sauce to cover its teeny tiny strands. If you're adamantly opposed to angel hair, use linguine, penne, or whatever pasta you love the most (any of them will do)!

8 ounces **angel hair pasta** or **linguine**

2 tablespoons plus 1 teaspoon **Cajun seasoning**

1 tablespoon plus 1 teaspoon **Lawry's Seasoned Salt**

½ pound **shrimp**, peeled and deveined

½ pound **mussels**, scrubbed and debearded

1 teaspoon **dried oregano**

1 teaspoon **onion powder**

1 teaspoon **garlic powder**

1 teaspoon **lemon pepper**

1 teaspoon **chili powder**

1 teaspoon **red pepper flakes**

½ teaspoon **kosher salt**

2 sticks (8 ounces) **unsalted butter**

1½ cups **fresh corn kernels**

Cloves from 2 heads **garlic**, minced

¼ **sweet onion**, diced

½ pound **andouille sausage**, thinly sliced on the diagonal

½ cup (packed) **fresh cilantro leaves**

2 **scallions**, thinly sliced

1   Bring a large pot of water to a boil. Cook the pasta according to the package directions. Reserving ¼ cup of the pasta water, drain the pasta and set aside.

2   Rinse the pot and fill it up with water again. Bring it to a boil over high heat. Once boiling, add the 2 tablespoons of the Cajun seasoning and the 1 tablespoon of the Lawry's seasoned salt. Carefully add the shrimp and mussels. When the shrimp turn opaque and curl up, after about 1 minute, remove them to a plate with tongs. When the mussels open wide, 2 to 4 minutes, remove them to the plate. Discard any mussels that do not open after 6 minutes.

3   In a small bowl, stir together the oregano, onion powder, garlic powder, lemon pepper, chili powder, pepper flakes, kosher salt, the remaining 1 teaspoon Lawry's seasoned salt,

and remaining 1 teaspoon Cajun seasoning. Set the spice mix aside.

4   Melt the butter in a large saucepan over medium heat. Once all the butter is melted, add the corn, garlic, and onion. Cook, stirring occasionally, until the onion is translucent and wilted, 3 to 4 minutes.

5   Stir the reserved spice mix and the sausage into the saucepan. Toss in the cooked pasta and make sure it is coated evenly. Add the seafood and toss again. Pour in the reserved pasta water, cover, and let it cook for 1 minute to meld the flavors. Toss one more time.

6   Transfer the pasta to a large bowl and garnish with the cilantro and scallions.

All the pop-ups I have ever done have been so special

cooking from the Internet to IRL, in real life. Goir

will show up for you at an event because they love you

lucky to experience the ultimate connection: taking

It's exciting for me to get real-time feedback and

to be said about the pop-up format,

restaurant or starting a

I didn't know

o me because they've allowed me to take my

viral is incredible, no doubt, but to know that people

cooking is unreal. I consider myself unbelievably

something you saw online into reality through food.

reactions when you try my dishes. There's something

too. Pop-ups are less commitment than owning a

catering service. When I was figuring it out,

what style of service I liked. I played

(In Real Life)
Pop-Ups IRL

around with casual-dining sushi and burgers as well as a sit-down restaurant style for my Chị Hai pop-up and Rising Chef series. These events have facilitated some of my most creative pursuits to date because I was able to imagine dishes with Jing Gao from Fly By Jing; Jimmy Ly, chef/owner of Madame Vo in New York City; and chef Alvin Cailan. In this chapter, you'll find a handful of my pop-up standbys like "The Shooketh Burger" (page 108) and Vietnamese Coffee Crème Brûlée (page 112).

Pickled Garlic Shrimp Ceviche

Prep Time: *3 hours 5 minutes*

Total Time: *3 hours 25 minutes*

Makes *a first course for 2 or a main course for 1*

I've been putting pickled garlic on my pho since I was a little kid. It's a staple Vietnamese topping, but I was shocked to find it's not commonly found in the United States. Chef J. Margaux of i.8Sushi approached me to create an @TwayDaBae sushi box. I felt like this was the perfect moment to highlight pickled garlic. Our first idea was to include it in a sushi roll, but the pickling liquid compromised the sushi's structure and made it too soggy. We settled on using garlic as a garnish. We later revisited the idea because I think pickled garlic is totally underrated. We needed a side dish that was quick and cost effective. Ceviche! It took a few revisions, but we nailed it: a delicious, easy seafood offering with pickled garlic as its headliner. You don't even have to turn on the stove for the shrimp because the acid from the lime juice will do all the "cooking" for you.

½ pound **shrimp,**
peeled and deveined

PICKLED GARLIC:

½ cup **distilled
white vinegar**

⅓ cup **sugar**

FOR SERVING:

¼ cup (packed)
fresh Thai basil or
basil leaves, cut into
chiffonade

½ cup **fresh lime juice**
(about 3 **limes**)

¼ cup **water**

Cloves from 1 head
garlic, thinly sliced

¼ cup (packed) **fresh
mint leaves,** cut
into chiffonade

**Rice puffs, tortilla
chips,** or **shrimp
chips**

1   Place the shrimp into a large bowl. Pour the
lime juice over the shrimp, cover with plastic
wrap, and refrigerate for at least 2 hours until
the shrimp has turned pink.

2   Meanwhile, make the pickled garlic: in a small
saucepan, whisk together the white vinegar,
sugar, and water. Set over medium heat and
stir until the sugar dissolves completely,
about 2 minutes. Once it comes to a simmer,
remove from the heat. Let the pickling liquid
cool to room temperature. Pour the liquid into
an airtight container, add the garlic, cover, and
refrigerate for at least 1 hour.

3   To serve: Drain the lime juice from the shrimp.
To the bowl with the shrimp, scoop in the
pickled garlic slices with a splash of the
pickling liquid. Mix in the basil and mint.

4   Transfer the ceviche to a serving bowl or
cup with a side of rice puffs, tortilla chips, or
shrimp chips.

Pickled Garlic Shrimp Ceviche, page 88

Tamarind Chicken Tenders

Prep Time: *1 hour 15 minutes*

Total Time: *2 hours*

Makes *a first course for 2 or main course for 1*

I competed at the 2022 TenderFest, a chicken tender cooking competition in Beverly Hills, California. I got to throw down with chefs Tim Hollingsworth, Nyesha Arrington, and Gregorio Stephenson. The prize was a trophy and bragging rights. Unfortunately, I didn't win the contest but I was really proud of what I made because it was another chance for my followers to try my food in real life. It's a winner to me and that's why I'm including it here for you to try at home. These tangy tamarind chicken tenders with my Bomb-Ass Ranch (page 178) is a flavor combo to be reckoned with. Who knew brown sugar and tamarind could be a power couple? My secret for success is a little bit of cayenne pepper in the buttermilk marinade and smoked paprika in the dredge for a perfect hint of smokiness.

(recipe continues)

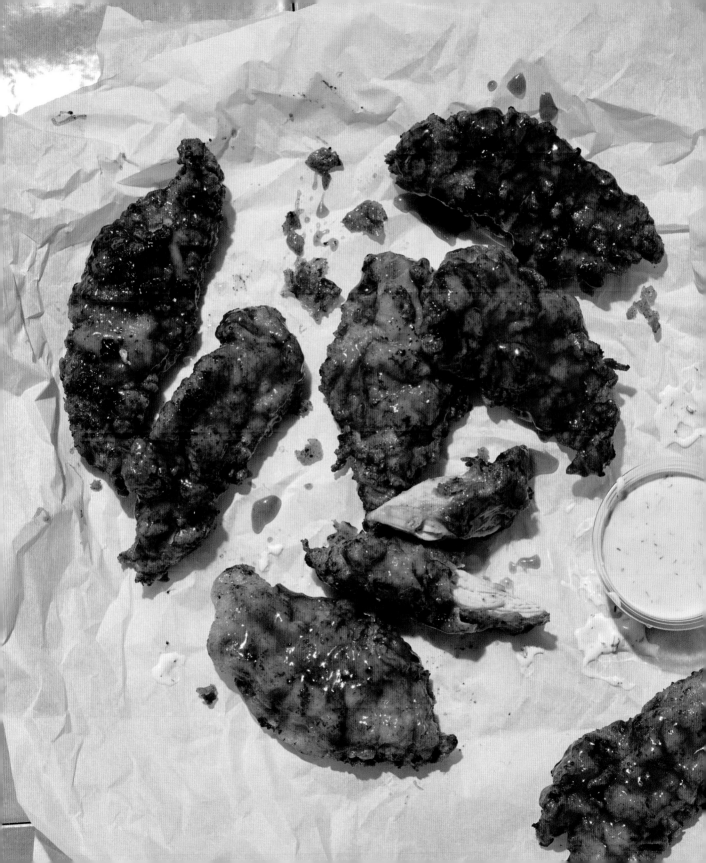

CHICKEN AND MARINADE:

½ pound **chicken tenders** or **chicken breasts**

1 cup **buttermilk**

1 tablespoon **garlic powder**

1 tablespoon **ground white pepper**

1 teaspoon **cayenne pepper**

TAMARIND GLAZE:

2 tablespoons **seedless tamarind paste**, torn into small pieces

¼ cup **hot water**

¼ cup **honey**

1½ tablespoons **oyster sauce**

1 tablespoon **soy sauce**

1 tablespoon **light brown sugar**

1 tablespoon **water**

1½ tablespoons **cornstarch**

Kosher salt

TO FINISH:

Vegetable oil, for deep-frying (about 2 quarts)

1 cup **all-purpose flour**

1 teaspoon **onion powder**

1 teaspoon **garlic powder**

1 teaspoon **cayenne pepper**

1 teaspoon **smoked paprika**

Bomb-Ass Ranch (page 178), for serving

1 Marinate the chicken: Place the chicken tenders in a large bowl or plastic zipper bag. If you're using chicken breast, cut each piece into 2-ounce pieces, lengthwise. In a small bowl, whisk together the buttermilk, garlic powder, white pepper, and cayenne. Pour the marinade over the chicken tenders and massage it in so each piece is coated. Seal the bag or cover the bowl with plastic wrap and refrigerate for at least 1 hour or up to overnight.

2 Make the glaze: In a small saucepan, combine the tamarind paste and hot water and bring to a boil over medium-high heat, breaking the tamarind up with a wooden spoon or heatproof whisk. Once the tamarind pulp is liquefied, remove from the heat. Carefully strain it through a fine-mesh sieve into a bowl and return it to the pan. Whisk in the honey, oyster sauce, soy sauce, brown sugar, and a pinch of salt until well combined. Reduce the heat to medium-low and cook the sauce until it starts to bubble, about 1 minute.

3 In a small dish, stir the 1 tablespoon water into the cornstarch to make a slurry. Stir the slurry into the tamarind mixture and let the glaze cook until it is glossy and thickened, 1 to 2 minutes longer. Remove from the heat.

4   To finish: Pour 2 inches vegetable oil into
a deep heavy pot and heat to 350°F over
medium-high heat, 6 to 8 minutes.

5   Meanwhile, in a bowl, whisk together the flour,
onion powder, garlic powder, cayenne, and
smoked paprika to make a dredge.

6   Nest a wire rack in a sheet pan. Drain the
marinade from the chicken. Generously coat
each chicken tender in the dredge until it is
completely coated with no chicken meat
exposed. Let the chicken tenders sit uncovered
on a wire rack for 5 minutes to let the dredge
adhere fully.

7   Nest another clean wire rack in a sheet pan and
set near the stove. Add the chicken tenders to
the oil and cook until they are golden brown
and reach an internal temperature of 165°F, 5 to
7 minutes. Transfer to the prepared wire rack
to drain.

8   Brush the tamarind glaze on the chicken
tenders. Transfer to a plate and enjoy with a
side of ranch dressing in a small bowl.

Grilled Pork Sausage

Nem Nướng

Prep Time: *20 minutes*

Total Time: *50 minutes*

Makes *6 patties*

Nem nướng are long, thin grilled Vietnamese pork sausage links. The @TwayDaBae version is shaped into Spam-like patties. I specifically chose pork belly for its higher fat content over loin or chop. The extra fat melts over the heat and the pork cooks in its own natural fat without using any added oil. I use pink curing salt, which is different from Himalayan pink salt. It helps quickly cure the pork and prevents the growth of microorganisms. The baking powder gives these patties a puffy, springy texture, unlike anything you've ever had. If you're not a sausage fan, I beg you to give my nem nướng a chance. My mom passed this recipe down to me and it hasn't failed me yet.

As part of my pop-up collaboration with Open Market, a neighborhood corner store in Los Angeles that specializes in sandwiches, I added my nem nướng to bánh mì. Paired with their in-house pâté and lemongrass aioli, it was bomb. Besides sandwiches, nem nướng works as a spring roll filling, protein for a vermicelli bowl, or on its own over a simple bowl of steamed rice.

¼ cup **diced pork fatback**

½ teaspoon **baking powder**

1 pound **ground pork belly**

1½ teaspoons **fish sauce**

1½ teaspoons **sugar**

¼ teaspoon **ground white pepper**

¼ teaspoon **pink curing salt**

¼ teaspoon **kosher salt**

1 tablespoon **minced shallot**

1½ teaspoons **minced garlic**

Canola oil

1 In a small saucepan, bring 2 cups water to a boil over medium-high heat. Add the pork fatback and cook until it turns opaque white and becomes fork-tender, about 10 minutes. Drain and let cool in a small bowl.

2 In a small dish, mix together the baking powder and 1½ teaspoons water.

3 In a food processor, combine the pork fatback, pork belly, fish sauce, sugar, white pepper, curing salt, kosher salt, and the baking powder mixture. Blend until the meat turns into a stiff paste that is sticky and springs back to the touch, 2 to 3 minutes. Scrape down the sides of the bowl with a spatula and continue to blend until it is completely smooth. Add the shallot and garlic and give it a few pulses more.

4 Transfer the paste to a large bowl. Coat your palms lightly with canola oil. Scoop up the paste and shape it into 6 Spam-like patties, weighing about 3 ounces each. Set aside on a plate.

5 To cook the sausage on the grill: Heat a grill to medium-high heat. Grill the patties for 2 to 3 minutes on each side, making sure to watch and move the patties away from flare-ups. They should feel firm to the touch and have an internal temperature of 165°F.

6 To cook the sausage on the stovetop: Preheat a skillet over medium heat for 2 minutes. Add the patties and pan-fry until golden brown and cooked through, 3 to 4 minutes per side. They should feel firm to the touch and have an internal temperature of 165°F.

7 Drain the nem nướng on a plate lined with paper towels and serve.

Crab Cellophane Noodles

Miến Xào Cua

Prep Time: *20 minutes*

Total Time: *30 minutes*

Makes *a main course for 2*

Miến is so underrated. (You've probably heard of them by other names, like cellophane noodles, glass noodles, mung bean noodles, vermicelli, or bean thread.) While the uninitiated would say they have no flavor, I treat them as a blank canvas where I can get creative with their fun, chewy texture. They've also gained international popularity as a healthier, gluten-free alternative to pasta and wheat-based noodles. Because miến soak up a lot of moisture, keep a little extra chicken stock on hand to keep them from drying out. When I make this at home for myself, I double up on the crab because I can! I recommend Dungeness crab, but if you can't find that, any freshly harvested lump crab will do.

4 ounces **mung bean cellophane noodles** (aka **bean thread**)

Hot water, for soaking

1 tablespoon **vegetable oil**

½ cup (packed) **Dungeness crabmeat**

1 tablespoon **oyster sauce**

1½ teaspoons **soy sauce**

1 teaspoon **sambal oelek**

2 **scallions**, thinly sliced

5 tablespoons **chicken stock**

1 teaspoon **sesame oil**

¼ cup (packed) **fresh cilantro leaves** (stems removed)

Freshly ground black pepper

1   In a small heatproof bowl, combine the cellophane noodles with enough hot water to cover and soak for 15 minutes to loosen the strands. Do not boil the noodles because they will fall apart. Drain the noodles.

2   Heat the vegetable oil in a large sauté pan over high heat until shimmering, about 1 minute. Add the crabmeat to the pan and stir until heated through, about 2 minutes.

3   Add the noodles and use tongs to toss with the crab. Continue to toss as you add the

oyster sauce, soy sauce, sambal, and scallions. Add the chicken stock and toss for another 2 minutes until it forms a light sauce. Remove from the heat.

4 Transfer the noodles to a large bowl. Finish the noodles with the sesame oil, cilantro, and a few pinches of black pepper.

Chicken Clay Pot

Prep Time: *10 minutes*

Total Time: *40 minutes*

Makes *a first course for 4 or main course for 2*

While I have several braised dishes in this book like Thịt Kho (page 42) and Cá Kho (page 35), chicken braised in a clay pot is my favorite. Clay pots are naturally porous and ensure the entire chicken and its juices are cooked in two ways: with direct heat and with moisture from the circulating steam inside. In Vietnamese, they're called *nồi đất* and they come in a variety of sizes. Imagine this: a bite of tender chicken soaked in its juices over rice. *chef's kiss*

I served chicken clay pot with crispy rice for a pop-up and guests raved about this course. I drew inspiration from comforting cơm cháy, a humble Vietnamese burnt rice typically served with braised meats. Try it out with my Viral Fried Rice (page 76) and a crispy fried egg.

- 4 **boneless, skin-on chicken thighs**
- 1 teaspoon **kosher salt**
- 1 teaspoon **freshly ground black pepper**
- 2 tablespoons or 1 cube **palm sugar**, plus more to taste
- 1 **medium shallot**, minced
- 6 **garlic cloves**, minced
- 2 tablespoons **fish sauce**, plus more to taste
- 1-inch knob **fresh ginger**, peeled and julienned
- 4 **scallions**, chopped
- 2 tablespoons **rice vinegar**
- **Viral Fried Rice** (page 76) or **Steamed White Rice** (page 26), for serving

1 Cut the chicken thighs into 1-inch pieces, season with the salt and pepper, and set aside.

2 In a 10-inch clay pot (or you can use a Dutch oven, too), melt the palm sugar over medium heat. Stir it constantly until it turns dark brown, 2 to 3 minutes.

3 Once you're happy with the color, stir in the shallot and garlic, then add the fish sauce and stir again.

4   When everything is combined, add the chicken and make sure the pieces are evenly coated. Stir in half the ginger and half the scallions. Reduce the heat to a simmer over medium–low heat, cover, and cook until the chicken is fully opaque, 10 to 15 minutes.

5   Stir in the rice vinegar and give the braising liquid a taste test. Adjust the seasoning with additional fish sauce or sugar to your taste.

6   Remove from the heat. You can serve the chicken out of your cooking vessel. You can also transfer the chicken and juices to a large bowl. Top it with the remaining ginger and scallions. Serve with a side of fried or steamed rice.

Chicken Porridge

Cháo Gà

Prep Time: *15 minutes*

Total Time: *2 hours 15 minutes*

Makes *a first course for 8 or a main course for 4*

Vietnamese tradition, especially my mom, says not to eat cháo gà during Lunar New Year celebrations because it's poor man's food and will stunt your flow of money for the year. I don't believe that! I served this chicken porridge at my New York City pop-up with Madame Vo in 2022. To me, cháo gà is a symbol of perseverance and appreciating what you have while working toward what you want. My mom loves to make this for parties, but I don't even need a party; I meal-prep it to have on hand for days. I use a whole chicken to make the flavorful broth, but some of the shredded meat can be used for the porridge and I reserve the rest for my Gỏi Gà (page 107). The leftovers taste even better as the rice absorbs all the gingery broth.

4-inch knob **fresh ginger**, peeled

1 **whole chicken** (3 to 4 pounds)

1 **yellow onion**, peeled and quartered

1 cup **jasmine rice**

2 tablespoons **fish sauce**, plus more to taste

Kosher salt

$\frac{1}{4}$ teaspoon **MSG** (optional)

Nước Mắm Gừng (page 174), for serving

1   Cut the ginger into small 1-inch pieces and smash with the side of a knife or with a rolling pin.

2   In a large pot, combine the whole chicken with enough water to cover by 1 inch. Bring to a boil over high heat and add the ginger and yellow onion. Reduce the heat to medium-low, cover,

and simmer until the chicken meat is opaque and the juices run clear when you cut it near the bone or the internal temperature of the chicken is 165°F, about 1$\frac{1}{2}$ hours.

3   Using tongs, transfer the chicken to a baking sheet and let cool for 20 minutes. Pull 1 cup of chicken meat off the bones and shred it with two forks. Cover and refrigerate the rest of the chicken for another use, such as Gỏi Gà (page 107).

4   Strain the stock through a fine-mesh sieve and discard the solids, making sure there are no bits in your stock. Measure out 10 cups of the stock and return it to the pot. Save any extra stock for other uses.

5   Bring the stock to a boil over high heat. Add the rice, reduce the heat to medium, and simmer the rice until tender and broken up, 30 to 40 minutes, stirring occasionally, so the bottom doesn't burn. The rice should be cooked through and considerably thicker. The longer you let the porridge cook, the thicker the consistency will be.

6   Stir in the reserved shredded chicken. Season the cháo gà with the fish sauce, a pinch of salt, and the MSG (if using). Taste and adjust with more salt or fish sauce before ladling it into soup bowls. Serve hot with a side of nước mắm gừng in a small bowl.

Chicken Slaw
Gỏi Gà

Prep Time: *20 minutes*
Total Time: *30 minutes*
Makes *a first course for 8*

I love to eat this chicken slaw with Cháo Gà (page 102), but I also enjoy it as a side salad or chicken slaw sandwich on a brioche bun with extra pickles. Rau răm (Vietnamese coriander) is a bit difficult to find, so regular fresh cilantro from the vegetable aisle will do just fine. But if you're lucky and can source rau răm, go for it because it really makes this dish sing. The unique sweet/salty/spicy/sour flavor of rau răm brings this from a basic slaw to a new Vietnamese classic that is both light and satisfying. Fried shallots add an umami crunch to every bite, and to be honest, ½ cup of them is only a suggestion. Add as much as your heart desires!

1 **whole boiled chicken** (see Cháo Gà, page 102)

1 **small red onion,** thinly sliced

1 cup (packed) **fresh Thai basil leaves,** cut into chiffonade

½ cup (packed) **fresh rau răm (Vietnamese coriander)** or **fresh cilantro,** roughly chopped with the soft stems

5 cups (packed) **shredded green cabbage**

½ cup **Fried Shallots** (page 194)

1 teaspoon **kosher salt,** plus more to taste

1 **lime,** halved

1 Take the chicken meat and skin (duh, the best part!) off the bones and shred with two forks.

2 In a big serving bowl, toss the chicken, red onion, Thai basil, rau răm, cabbage, and fried shallots together. Season the slaw with the salt and lime juice to taste. Toss it one more time. Taste and adjust to your liking with more lime or salt.

"The Shooketh Burger"

Prep Time: *35 minutes*
Total Time: *1 hour 40 minutes*
Makes *4 burgers*

"The Shooketh Burger" came to life with the help of chefs Alvin Cailan and Christian Alquiza. They asked to collaborate on a burger for the Amboy Burger Club and I had to ask myself, "How can I make a Vietnamese burger?" I decided to pay homage to my favorite beef dish, Bò Lúc Lắc (page 32). Bò lúc lắc is cubes of steak marinated in a savory soy glaze, seared on high heat while being tossed vigorously with veggies like onions and peppers. I took the soy marinade and cooked it down until it became thick enough to be a glaze. Onions and peppers became a sofrito-ish puree that I used as a dressing for the watercress. To tie it all together, we made a black pepper garlic lime mayonnaise and served it with a side of Amboy fries. And thus "The Shooketh Burger" was born! It is so good, it leaves you shook (like the trending meme at the time). Not trying to toot my own horn here, but *toot toot* this burger is truly a work of art. If you really want to kick it up a notch, add some pickled onions to this dish so it'll hit all the flavor profiles and make the burger even more savory.

(recipe continues)

SOFRITO PUREE:

1 **red bell pepper,** thinly sliced

½ **yellow onion,** thinly sliced

4 **garlic cloves,** peeled but whole

2 tablespoons **mirin**

2 tablespoons **rice vinegar**

1 tablespoon **soy sauce**

Kosher salt and **freshly ground black pepper**

BLACK PEPPER LIME AIOLI:

1 cup **Kewpie mayonnaise**

4 **garlic cloves,** minced

2 tablespoons **fresh lime juice**

4½ teaspoons **freshly ground black pepper**

GLAZE:

2 tablespoons **sugar**

1 tablespoon **oyster sauce**

1 tablespoon **Maggi liquid seasoning**

1 tablespoon **honey**

1 teaspoon **grated garlic**

1 teaspoon **garlic powder**

1 teaspoon **sambal oelek**

½ teaspoon **sesame oil**

BURGERS:

2 cups **pickle brine** (from **Đồ Chua,** page 191)

Kosher salt

1 **red onion,** thinly sliced

1¾ pounds **ground beef**

Vegetable oil, for pan-frying

Freshly ground black pepper

4 slices **provolone cheese**

4 **brioche buns,** split horizontally and toasted

2 cups packed **watercress**

1   Make the sofrito puree: Heat a saucepan over medium-high heat for 1 minute. Add the bell pepper, yellow onion, and garlic. Cook, stirring occasionally, until they are soft and tender, 8 to 10 minutes.

2   Using tongs, carefully transfer everything to a blender. Add the mirin, vinegar, and soy sauce and blend the vegetables until it forms a smooth sauce, 1 to 2 minutes. Taste and adjust the seasoning to your liking with salt and pepper.

3   Make the black pepper lime aioli: In a small bowl, stir together the mayonnaise, garlic, lime juice, and black pepper. Mix well and set aside.

4   Make the glaze: In a small saucepan, whisk together the sugar, oyster sauce, Maggi seasoning, honey, grated garlic, garlic powder, sambal, and sesame oil. Set the pan over medium-low heat and cook down, stirring occasionally, until it turns into a thick glaze, about 15 minutes. Transfer the glaze to a heatproof container and set aside to cool.

5   Make the burgers: At least 30 minutes before assembling the burgers, whisk together the pickle brine and 1 tablespoon salt in a pint jar or container until the salt dissolves. Add the red onion and set aside.

6   Divide the ground beef into 8 balls, each weighing about $3\frac{1}{2}$ ounces.

7   Preheat a cast-iron skillet over high heat. Add enough vegetable oil to coat the bottom and once the oil is smoking, place 2 balls of meat in the pan 3 inches apart and use a metal press or heavy spatula to flatten the balls down to thin patties $\frac{1}{3}$ inch thick. Cook until they develop a nice char, about 2 minutes. Season the top sides with a generous pinch of salt and pepper.

8   Flip the patties over and split 1 tablespoon of the glaze over both. Add a slice of provolone to one patty and let sizzle undisturbed 1 to 2 minutes more. Use a spatula to stack the plain patty over the patty with cheese.

9   Spread the pepper mayo on both sides of each brioche bun. Place the meat patty stack on the bottom bun.

10 Cook the remaining burgers in the same way, adding more vegetable oil to the pan for every round.

11 In a small bowl, mix the watercress with 2 tablespoons of the sofrito puree. Place the rest of the sofrito puree in a small bowl to add more to your burger, or use it as a dip for fries. Divide the salad among the 4 stacked burgers and add a few slices of pickled onion. Complete the burgers with their top buns.

Vietnamese Coffee Crème Brûlée

Prep Time: *1 hour 20 minutes*
Total Time: *2 hours 20 minutes*
Makes *a dessert for 4*

Crème brûlée was the first dessert I learned to make in culinary school and it just kinda . . . stuck with me. I've also never met a coffee dessert that I didn't like. Why not the both of them together? I'm gonna be real: I didn't get a chance to fully develop and test the recipe until the Covid-19 lockdown happened. While I was isolating, I took advantage of being at home to finally explore the ideas that I didn't have time for—which led to me sharing recipes online with all of you. It took me four tries to perfect this recipe and get the strong coffee flavor to shine through. Since I was posting this online, I needed it to also be easy enough for anyone to re-create. It turned out to be a hit on TikTok and Instagram! I've kept this dessert as a repeat offering on almost all my pop-up menus. You will need some special tools like a torch and ramekins to make these crème brûlées, but once you have them, you can make them anytime you have a craving.

(recipe continues)

6 **large egg yolks**

⅓ cup brewed
Vietnamese coffee
(for how to brew,
see Egg Coffee,
page 199), chilled

½ teaspoon **kosher
salt**

2 cups **heavy cream**

⅓ cup plus
4 teaspoons **sugar**

1   Preheat the oven to 350°F.

2   In a small bowl, whisk together the egg yolks, coffee, and salt. Set aside.

3   In a saucepan, heat the heavy cream gradually over medium heat. Whisk ⅓ cup of the sugar into the heavy cream and remove from the heat when it begins to simmer, about 2 minutes.

4   Working one ladle at a time, slowly whisk the warm heavy cream into the egg yolk mixture until it is uniform.

5   Divide the mixture among four 6-ounce ramekins. Place the filled ramekins in a baking dish or roasting pan with high sides and add water to come halfway up the ramekins. Carefully place it onto the middle rack of the oven and bake until the custard is set and toasted a light brown on top, about 50 minutes.

6   Carefully remove the ramekins from the baking dish and let cool for 15 minutes. Pour out the water and set the ramekins on a sheet pan. Chill the custards uncovered in the fridge for at least 1 hour.

7   Once well chilled, evenly sprinkle 1 teaspoon sugar over each custard. Set the ramekins still on the sheet pan on the stove. Using a kitchen torch, carefully flame the sugar in a circular motion until the sugar browns and bubbles into a toasty sugar shell. (Alternatively, broil the ramekins on the highest rack in a preheated oven until caramelized and bubbling, 3 to 4 minutes.)

8   Carefully remove from the oven and let cool until the sugar hardens and stops actively bubbling.

I developed this recipe for my pop-up with the spice queen herself, Jing Gao, the owner and founder of Fly By Jing (who makes the best chili crisp on the market). Inspired by her love of sweet and savory flavor combinations, I thought our collab needed a special dessert that pays homage to her crisps—but I had no idea that we would end up with something like this! We wanted to take an ordinary dish of ice cream as a base and combine it with chili crisp. However, something was missing: I wanted to add a peanut brittle for texture. And why would I stick with a regular recipe when I can try to make a fish sauce brittle? It took me four tries to get the brittle the way I had envisioned it. I wanted it to look like a proper brittle, a beautiful golden brown, and not too sticky or chewy. I couldn't be happier with the final product and I'm curious to see what ice cream flavors you try with this! Then again, it's a yummy treat on its own, too.

Fish Sauce Brittle

Prep Time: *1 hour 5 minutes*
Total Time: *1 hour 35 minutes*
Makes *1 pound 10 ounces*

(recipe continues)

1½ cups **sugar**

⅓ cup **light corn syrup**

2½ cups unsalted **dry-roasted peanuts**

¼ cup **fish sauce**

1 teaspoon **baking soda**

1 teaspoon **vanilla extract**

1 Line a sheet pan with parchment paper.

2 In a saucepan, stir together the sugar, ¾ cup water, and the corn syrup. Clip a candy thermometer on the side of the pan, set over medium-high heat, and bring the sugar to a soft ball stage (230° to 245°F). When it reaches 240°F in about 15 minutes, it will develop rapid, white bubbles. At this point, fold in the peanuts. Bring the peanut mixture to a hard crack stage, 300° to 310°F, stirring constantly so the sugar doesn't burn. It will turn a light tan color and should take 10 to 12 minutes.

3 Carefully add the fish sauce and mix until it's well combined. Add the baking soda and the vanilla and continue to stir until everything comes together and puffs up and is an opaque light brown.

4 Carefully pour the mixture onto the prepared sheet pan. With an offset spatula or the back of a spoon, spread the brittle flat. Be careful not to touch it, the sugar is very hot.

5 Place it in the fridge for 30 minutes or leave it out at room temperature for 1 hour for it to harden. When it has cooled off and is hard, crack it into pieces. Store the brittle in an airtight container for up to 1 month.

Gorgeous gorgeous girls love soup! It's not an exaggerati[on]

soups very seriously. I mean, after all, our most iconi[c]

doesn't take an advanced palate to enjoy them. Whether

there's a soup out there for everyone. I'm excited t[o]

dishes. Fill up your kitchen with the

If you're adventurous and willi[ng]

when I tell you that we Vietnamese take our

dishes are soups. Soups can do no wrong and it

you're into rich savory broths or just a light base,

also show you how I've put twists on otherwise basic

intoxicating aromas of an iconic phở or beefy bún bò huế.

to try a quintessential, but understated, Vietnamese

bowl, try my hearty canh khổ qua.

SOUPS

Sour Tomato Egg Drop Soup

Canh Trúng Cà Chua

Prep Time: *15 minutes*

Total Time: *25 minutes*

Makes *a first course for 8 or main course for 4*

My egg drop soup is a little different from the kind you would order at a Chinese restaurant. Tomatoes are softened with aromatics and then seasoned with a rich chicken stock and fish sauce. In the end, beaten eggs cook very quickly as they swirl around the hot soup becoming tasty wisps to slurp up. It's incredibly easy to prepare, especially if you're having a busy day and need a complete, nourishing meal.

1 tablespoon **vegetable oil**

2 **garlic cloves,** minced

1 **shallot,** minced

4 **Roma (plum) tomatoes,** cut into wedges

4 cups **chicken stock**

3 tablespoons **fish sauce**

2 tablespoons **sugar**

1 teaspoon **chicken bouillon powder**

5 tablespoons **rice vinegar**

2 **large eggs,** beaten

2 **scallions,** thinly sliced

¼ cup (packed) **fresh cilantro leaves** (stems removed)

Freshly ground black pepper

1 Heat the vegetable oil in a soup pot over medium heat until shimmering, about 2 minutes. Add the garlic and shallot and cook, stirring until the garlic is golden, 3 to 4 minutes. Add the tomato wedges and cook, stirring until they wilt a bit, about 2 minutes longer.

2 Add the chicken stock to the pot and bring it to a boil. Once boiling, reduce the heat to a simmer and season the soup with the fish sauce, sugar, chicken bouillon powder, and vinegar.

3 Stream the beaten eggs slowly into the pot while swirling the soup with a chopstick or ladle so you can create ribbons of eggs.

4 Divide the soup among bowls. Garnish each bowl with the scallions, cilantro, and a pinch of black pepper.

We don't talk about the benefits of beets enough. I mean, come on, they're sweet, tender when cooked through, and have a handful of nutritional benefits. They're great for helping lower blood pressure and contain iron, which is vital for your body's development. Not to mention beets dye the entire soup bright pink! A soup that is tasty, good for you, and . . . cute? Stop! To bring it all together, you can use water, chicken stock, or vegetable broth (which I personally think brings out the best flavor).

Beet Soup

Prep Time: *10 minutes*

Total Time: *1 hour 10 minutes*

Makes *a first course for 4 or main course for 2*

1 tablespoon **vegetable oil**

4 **garlic cloves**, minced

½ pound **ground pork**

10 cups **vegetable broth, chicken stock**, or **water**

3 medium **beets**, peeled and cut into 1-inch cubes

1 **carrot**, peeled and cut into 1-inch cubes

1 **Yukon Gold potato**, peeled and cut into 1-inch cubes

1 tablespoon **fish sauce**

½ teaspoon **sugar**

¼ cup (packed) **fresh cilantro leaves** (stems removed)

Freshly cracked black pepper

1   Heat the vegetable oil in a medium soup pot over medium heat until shimmering, 1 to 2 minutes. Add the garlic and cook, stirring until it turns golden, about 1 minute. Add the ground pork and stir, breaking it up with a wooden spoon, until it turns from pink to light brown, 3 to 4 minutes.

2   Add the broth, beets, carrot, and potato. Increase the heat to medium-high to bring to a boil. Reduce to a simmer over medium-low heat, stirring occasionally until the beets and potatoes are fork-tender, about 40 minutes.

3   Season the soup with the fish sauce and sugar. Taste and adjust it to your liking. Transfer the soup to a large serving bowl. Garnish with the cilantro and a pinch of black pepper.

Squash Soup

Prep Time: *15 minutes*

Total Time: *45 minutes*

Makes *a first course for 4 or main course for 2*

Squash is one of those vegetables that is available at grocery stores year-round. With a simple base of garlic and ground pork, kabocha squash transforms from a hearty gourd into a buttery-soft sweet soup. It doesn't hurt that the soup is quick and easy to make, too.

1 medium **kabocha squash**

2 tablespoons **vegetable oil**

4 **garlic cloves**, minced

½ pound **ground pork**

4 cups **chicken stock** or **water**

1 teaspoon **fish sauce**

Kosher salt and **freshly cracked black pepper**

2 **scallions**, thinly sliced

4 sprigs **fresh cilantro**, leaves picked

1   Cut the stem off the kabocha squash and discard the stem. Slice the squash in half and clean out the guts with a spoon. Slice each half into even 1-inch-wide wedges. Cut the wedges into smaller 1-inch chunks.

2   Heat the vegetable oil in a medium soup pot over medium-high heat until shimmering, about 2 minutes. Add the garlic and pork, breaking up the pork with a wooden spoon, and cook, stirring, until the pork is no longer pink, 2 to 3 minutes.

3   Carefully pour the chicken stock into the pot and bring it to a boil. Reduce the heat to a simmer, add the squash pieces, stirring to make sure they are submerged, cover, and cook, stirring periodically, until the squash is fork-tender, 15 to 20 minutes.

4   Season with the fish sauce and adjust the seasoning to your liking with salt and pepper. Transfer the soup to a serving bowl. Sprinkle the scallions and cilantro leaves over the soup and serve hot.

Vietnamese Sour Soup

Canh Chua

Prep Time: *40 minutes*
Total Time: *1 hour 20 minutes*
Makes *a first course for 8 or main course for 4*

When I was nineteen, my mom taught me how to make canh chua, my first-ever Vietnamese soup. The soups in Vietnam are served family-style in a big bowl for everyone to ladle into their own bowl. It's almost like getting a side of soup in the United States, but everyone is served. You want your canh chua to have a good balance of sour from the tamarind, sweet from the pineapple, and salty from the fish sauce without one element overpowering the rest. I suggest catfish, but salmon is a great alternative. You also have the option of using chicken stock or water, but I go for the stock every time because it makes the soup so flavorful. Check your local Asian supermarket for rice paddy herb (ngò ôm) and green elephant ear (taro) stems. If you have no luck finding them, you can omit the rice paddy herb and substitute celery (my arch nemesis! I hate the smell, but you do you) for the elephant ear stems.

4 tablespoons **fish sauce**, plus more to taste

1 tablespoon plus 1 teaspoon **sugar**, plus more to taste

Pinch of **cayenne pepper**

Freshly ground black pepper

4 **catfish steaks** or **fillets** (4 ounces each)

6 tablespoons seedless **tamarind paste**, torn into small pieces

½ cup boiling **water**

1 tablespoon **avocado oil**

5 **garlic cloves**, minced

3 **Roma (plum) tomatoes**, quartered

6 cups **chicken stock** or **water**

2 tablespoons **soy sauce**

2 **elephant ear (taro) stems**, peeled and cut into 1-inch pieces

½ cup cubed fresh **pineapple**

½ pound **okra** (optional), sliced crosswise on the diagonal

2 tablespoons **distilled white vinegar**, plus more to taste

½ pound **mung bean sprouts**

1 cup (packed) **fresh ngò ôm (rice patty herb**, optional), cut into 1-inch pieces with the stems

1 In a shallow bowl, combine 2 tablespoons of the fish sauce, 1 tablespoon of the sugar, the cayenne, and a pinch of black pepper. Add the catfish, flipping it a few times to make sure all the pieces are coated. Cover and refrigerate for 15 minutes if you are in a hurry or 30 minutes for the full flavor to develop.

2 In a small heatproof bowl, mix the tamarind paste with the boiling water. Stir until the paste dissolves into the water. Strain it through a fine-mesh sieve. Set it aside.

3 Heat the avocado oil in a large soup pot over medium heat until shimmering, about 1 minute. Add the garlic to the pot and cook, stirring, until it turns golden, 1 to 2 minutes. Add a few pieces of tomato and mash them up.

4 Stir in the chicken stock, soy sauce, strained tamarind paste, and the remaining 2 tablespoons fish sauce and 1 teaspoon sugar. Carefully lower the catfish into the soup.

5 Cover and simmer until the fish is no longer pink and looks opaque white, 2 to 3 minutes. Transfer the fish to a plate to avoid overcooking it.

6 Add the remaining tomatoes, the elephant ear stems, pineapple, and okra (if using). Increase the heat to medium-high and bring it to a boil. Reduce to a simmer and cook until the tomatoes soften and the elephant ear stems are tender, about 10 minutes.

7 Stir in the vinegar. Adjust the soup with more fish sauce, vinegar, or sugar. Add the bean sprouts and rice patty herb (if using).

8 Divide the soup among bowls and top each with a piece of catfish.

Bitter Melon Soup

Canh Khổ Qua

Prep Time: *20 minutes*
Total Time: *1 hour 35 minutes*
Makes *a main course for 8*

I know bitter melon soup is divisive: You will either wholeheartedly love it or you simply will not be a fan. It doesn't seem like there is any in-between! I don't blame people for not loving it, though, because bitter melon is an acquired taste but I happen to think it is soooo good. When I was a kid, I used to pretend to like bitter melon to impress my mom. But, ha, the joke's on me because I genuinely grew to enjoy it. I served this dish at my Lunar New Year pop-up at Madame Vo in New York City because *canh khổ qua* directly translates to "hardship passed." For the upcoming year, it promises the passing of hardships, and that your difficulties don't last long (if at all!).

3 tablespoons **dried wood ear mushrooms**

Hot water, for soaking

2 ounces **mung bean cellophane noodles** (aka **bean thread**)

½ pound **ground pork**

2 teaspoons **chicken bouillon powder**

1 tablespoon **fish sauce,** plus more to taste

1 teaspoon **MSG** (optional)

4 **bitter melons**

2 quarts **chicken stock**

2 **scallions,** thinly sliced

½ cup (packed) **fresh cilantro leaves** (stems removed)

Freshly cracked black pepper

Steamed White Rice (optional; page 26), for serving

1. In a heatproof bowl, combine the wood ear mushrooms with hot water to cover and soak until the mushrooms have grown triple their size, about 10 minutes. When the water is cool enough to handle, rub the mushrooms lightly to remove any grit and drain off the water. Pat the wood ears dry with a paper towel.

2. Meanwhile, in a large heatproof bowl, combine the cellophane noodles with enough hot water to cover, and soak until the noodles are soft, about 2 minutes. Drain the noodles and set aside until the wood ears are softened. Hold onto the large bowl.

3. Mince the noodles and wood ear mushrooms together. Return them to the large bowl and mix with the ground pork. Season the pork mixture with the chicken bouillon powder, fish sauce, and MSG (if using). Mix it once more and set aside.

4. Cut the ends off each bitter melon. Cut each bitter melon crosswise into 2-inch lengths. Remove the spongy white center by scraping it out with a spoon or cut it out carefully with a paring knife.

5. In a medium soup pot, bring the chicken stock to a boil over high heat.

6. Meanwhile, stuff the bitter melon pieces with the meat mixture.

7. Once the chicken stock comes to a boil, carefully add the stuffed bitter melon to the pot. Reduce the heat to medium-low, cover, and simmer the soup until the color of the bitter melon changes from a bright green to a mossy green, 30 to 40 minutes. The longer you let it simmer the less bitter it will be, but don't cook it for more than 1 hour because the bitter melon will fall apart.

8. Remove from the heat and season the soup with more fish sauce, if needed, adding little by little and tasting as you go until you are happy with it.

9. Carefully transfer the soup to a serving bowl. Garnish it with the scallions, cilantro, and a few pinches of black pepper. Enjoy the soup by itself or with a side of steamed rice.

Bánh Canh Cua, page 132

Crab Udon

Bánh Canh Cua

Prep Time: *15 minutes*

Total Time: *45 minutes*

Makes *a main course for 4*

I wanted to capture the explosive flavor of crab somehow. Homemade, slurp-worthy udon noodles are perfect for bánh canh cua's thicker soup base. Damn, I love crab. I think its meat is the most flavorful compared to other shellfish, and it's available in such a wide range of flavors and textures. I know that making noodles from scratch sounds like a lot of work, but I promise it's very straightforward and worth the time you put into it. My trick for udon noodles is to use an adjustable potato ricer with large holes. You'll get shorter udon pieces that you can slurp up with a spoon. You can also use a piping bag for longer, more traditional looking udon.

UDON NOODLES:

1 cup **rice flour**

1 tablespoon **vegetable oil**

$\frac{1}{2}$ teaspoon **kosher salt**

1 cup **tapioca starch**

SOUP:

$\frac{3}{4}$ cup **vegetable oil**

1 tablespoon **annatto seeds**

3 tablespoons **minced shallot**

1 pound **shell-on crab claws**

6 cups **chicken stock**

1 tablespoon **fish sauce**

1 tablespoon **chicken bouillon powder**

Kosher salt and **freshly cracked black pepper**

1 tablespoon **minced garlic**

1 pound **fresh lump crabmeat**

2 **scallions,** thinly sliced

$\frac{1}{4}$ cup (packed) **fresh cilantro leaves** (stems removed)

1 Make the udon noodles: In a microwave-safe bowl, stir together the rice flour, 1½ cups water, the vegetable oil, and salt. Microwave for 2 minutes. (Alternatively, heat the mixture in a small pot over low heat until it turns into a loose white slurry, about 5 minutes.) Give it a good mix with a heatproof spatula. Off the heat, add the tapioca starch and stir until it becomes a paste.

2 Bring a medium pot of water to a boil over high heat. Prepare a bowl of cold water nearby.

3 Place half the udon noodle mixture in a potato ricer fitted with large holes and press it slowly to release noodles into the boiling water. Boil until they float, about 2 minutes. Take the noodles out with a slotted spoon and place into the bowl of cold water until you're ready to serve. Repeat with the other half of the udon dough. You can also make longer noodles with a piping bag, but I think a potato ricer is faster.

4 Make the soup: In a small saucepan, combine ½ cup of the vegetable oil and the annatto seeds and heat over medium heat until they start to bubble, about 3 minutes. Remove from the heat and cool for 10 minutes. The oil will turn bright red as it steeps. Strain it into a small bowl and set aside.

5 Heat 2 tablespoons of the vegetable oil (or enough oil to coat the bottom) in a large soup pot over medium heat until shimmering, about 1 minute. Add 2 tablespoons of the shallot and the crab claws. Stir until the claws turn orange and the shallots soften, about 5 minutes.

6 Pour the chicken stock into the pot, increase the heat to high, and bring it to a boil. Reduce the heat to medium-low, season with the fish sauce and chicken bouillon powder. Adjust the seasoning to your liking with salt and pepper. Set the soup over low heat to keep it warm.

7 Heat the remaining 2 tablespoons vegetable oil in a pan over medium heat until shimmering, about 1 minute. Add the remaining 1 tablespoon shallot, the garlic, and lump crab and cook until the shallots soften slightly, about 2 minutes. Drizzle 1 tablespoon of annatto oil over the lump crab for some color. Taste it and season with salt and pepper, if needed. Remove from the heat.

8 Divide the udon noodles and crab claws among four bowls. Add a ladle of broth and a few generous spoons of the crabmeat. Garnish each bowl with the scallions, cilantro, and a pinch of black pepper. Finish with a drizzle of the annatto oil.

Spicy Beef Noodles

Bún Bò Huế

Prep Time: *15 minutes*
Total Time: *4 hours 20 minutes*
Makes *4 large bowls*

When you think of Vietnamese cuisine, phở is one of the first dishes that comes to mind. Bún bò huế (BBH) is an underdog noodle dish, but is equally delicious. It's got umami from the fish sauce, a savory ham and beef broth, sweetness from pineapple, and a spicy base of Lemongrass Saté (page 181). It's my comfort meal when I'm craving something spicy, salty, and delicious. One of the key differences between phở and BBH are the noodles. For this recipe, you'll need to buy a thicker vermicelli that can better absorb all the flavors in this dish. When you head to the market, look for "giant tay" or "jianxi rice stick" on the label. My BBH features banana blossoms, which are cone-shaped flowers that grow at the end of a banana cluster. They have a slightly bitter taste and a texture similar to artichoke hearts. You also can't forget chả lụa (aka "Vietnamese ham"), which is a pork roll made with garlic and fish sauce that is wrapped in banana leaves or bark and steamed. If you have any left over, you can enjoy it as a snack or as another protein with rice.

4 **fresh lemongrass stalks**

½ pound **boneless beef shank** or **chuck**

6 **unsmoked ham hocks**

2 tablespoons **vegetable oil**

¼ cup **minced garlic**

¼ cup **minced shallot**

2 **fresh Thai bird's eye chilies,** chopped

1 tablespoon **Lemongrass Saté** (page 181)

1 **yellow onion,** peeled and quartered

½ cup **fresh pineapple** chunks

3 tablespoons **fish sauce,** plus more to taste

2 teaspoons **shrimp paste**

2 to 3 medium pieces **rock sugar** or 2 to 3 tablespoons **sugar,** to taste

14 ounces **thick rice vermicelli noodles**

12 ounces **chà lụa,** wrapping removed and thinly sliced

1 **red onion,** sliced

1 **banana blossom,** thinly sliced

1 **head cabbage,** thinly sliced

5 **limes,** cut into wedges

1 bunch **Thai basil,** stems removed

1 Remove the dry outermost layer from each lemongrass stalk. Trim the top 5 inches and 1 inch from the bottom root end, leaving you with a tender white center. Bruise the stalks with a pestle, rolling pin, or bottom of a pot. Mince 1 stalk and set aside.

2 In a large soup pot, combine the beef shank, ham hocks, and enough water to cover. Bring to a boil over high heat and cook until the beef turns opaque and the water looks murky, 5 to 8 minutes. Remove the meats and rinse with cold water to remove any blood or solids. Discard the water and clean out the pot.

3 Preheat a skillet over medium heat. Add the vegetable oil and heat until shimmering, about 2 minutes. Add the garlic, shallot, chilies, and minced lemongrass and cook, stirring often, until the shallots soften, 2 to 3 minutes. Stir the lemongrass saté into the mixture and cook until combined and aromatic, about 2 minutes longer. Transfer the mixture to a small bowl and set aside to cool.

4 In the soup pot, combine 10 cups water, the ham hocks, beef shank, yellow onion, pineapple, and the remaining 3 lemongrass stalks. Bring to a boil over high heat, then reduce to low heat and simmer until the ham hocks are tender, about 45 minutes. Remove the ham hocks to a plate and cover with plastic wrap to prevent them from drying out.

(recipe continues)

5 Skim off any impurities that might have risen to the top of the broth. Add the garlic mixture to the pot, cover, and simmer until the beef shank is tender, about 2 hours.

6 Carefully transfer the beef shank to a cutting board. Slice it thinly, transfer it to a plate, and cover it with plastic wrap.

7 Simmer the broth for another 2 hours. About 5 minutes before the end of the cooking time, season the soup with the fish sauce, shrimp paste, and rock sugar. Taste and adjust with more fish sauce or sugar, if needed.

8 Remove from the heat and carefully strain out the aromatics. Return the broth to the pot, add the ham hocks, cover, and keep warm over low heat.

9 Cook the rice vermicelli noodles according to the package directions.

10 Arrange the cabbage, limes, and Thai basil on a platter.

11 Divide the noodles among four large bowls. Arrange 4 or 5 slices of chả lụa, a few slices of beef, a ham hock, a red onion slice, and a few pieces of banana blossom. Ladle 2 to 2½ cups of the warmed broth to cover the noodles.

Kevin's Phở

Prep Time: *45 minutes*
Total Time: *6 hours 15 minutes*
Makes *8 large bowls*

Kevin is my stepdad, who happens to be an amazing cook. And I'm proud of his phở. His recipe is special to my entire family and it's the only entry in this book that isn't completely mine. I did not make any changes to it because I genuinely think it's perfect as it is. In 2019, this bowl of phở singlehandedly saved my family's Vietnamese restaurant in Thousand Oaks, California, from closing. All bias aside: This is, hands down, the best phở I've ever tasted.

In my experience, most people tend to be extremely tight-lipped about their phở recipes. I'm incredibly honored and grateful that Kevin shared his secrets with me, and now, with you. He thinks if you're going to go through all the trouble of making phở yourself, at the very least, you should know how to do it right. I promise, if you follow Kevin's wisdom, you'll soon be a phở-fessional.

Phở is the most famous dish from Vietnam, and now you can find it all over the world! It is made with a super-savory broth that is simmered for hours with either beef bones or chicken bones and tons of warm spices like cinnamon, ginger, and star anise. The best phở broths will be rich and full of flavor, not bland, salty, or greasy. (Kevin also uses a secret umami booster: Cốt Phở Bò brand "beef-flavored phở soup base.") This treasured broth is then poured over rice noodles and slices of tender meat. It's crowned with crunchy bean sprouts, fresh herbs, lime, and spicy chilies.

(recipe continues)

BEEF BROTH:

10 pounds **beef bones**

6 tablespoons **kosher salt**

1 pound **flank steak**, left whole

1 pound **beef brisket**, left whole

5 **cardamom pods**

3 **cinnamon sticks**

5 whole **star anise**

2 tablespoons **whole cloves**

1 tablespoon **coriander seeds**

2½ teaspoons **fennel seeds**

6-inch knob **fresh ginger**

1 large **yellow onion**

2 large **shallots**

¾ cup **rock sugar** or **granulated sugar**, plus more to taste

7 tablespoons **mushroom bouillon powder**, plus more to taste

¼ cup plus 2 teaspoons **Cốt Phở Bò Beef-Flavored Phở Soup Base**

3 bunches **scallions**, white parts reserved and green parts thinly sliced

FOR SERVING:

16 ounces **phở noodles** or **medium rice noodles**

3 bunches **fresh cilantro**, chopped with tender stems

2 **limes**, quartered

½ pound **mung bean sprouts**

4 **jalapeños**, thinly sliced

1 batch **pickled garlic** from Pickled Garlic Shrimp Ceviche (page 88)

1. Make the beef broth: In a large stockpot, combine the beef bones, 10 quarts water, and 1 tablespoon of the salt and bring to a boil over high heat. Once it boils, remove from the heat and rinse the bones with cold water. Clean the pot out.

2. Return the cleaned beef bones to the stock pot and add 10 quarts water and the remaining 5 tablespoons salt. Take note of the water level, you'll need to know this later. Add the flank steak and brisket and bring to a boil over high heat. Reduce the heat to medium-low, cover, and simmer for 4 hours. Skim off any impurities that float to the top.

3. Smash the cardamom pods and cinnamon sticks in a mortar and pestle or on a cutting board with the bottom of a pot to release their flavors. Set a dry skillet over high heat. When it starts smoking, immediately reduce the heat to low. Toast the cardamom and cinnamon until you start to smell it, 2 to 3 minutes. Add the star anise, cloves, coriander seeds, and fennel seeds. Continue to stir and toast until they are fragrant, 30 seconds to 1 minute. Carefully transfer the toasted spices to a heatproof bowl to cool. Wrap the spices in a cheesecloth and tie it closed or use a tea ball.

4   If you have a gas stove, carefully roast the ginger, onion, and shallots over the open flame with tongs until their outsides are burnt. (Alternatively, broil the ginger, yellow onion, and shallots on a sheet pan until their skins are burnt, turning occasionally with tongs, about 5 minutes per side.) Place the ginger, onion, and shallots into a large bowl and wash with cold water to remove some of the char. Smash the ginger to release its flavor. Peel the onion and shallots.

5   Remove the beef bones from the pot with tongs and discard. Cover the brisket and flank steak with more water to bring it back up to the original 10-quart level. Stir in the rock sugar, mushroom bouillon powder, and beef-flavored phở soup base. Increase the heat to high and bring to a boil again.

6   Skim the broth for impurities. Add the yellow onion, ginger, shallots, scallion whites, and the spice pouch. Reduce the heat to medium-low and simmer for 30 minutes.

7   Taste and adjust the seasoning to your liking. If it's too sweet, add more mushroom bouillon powder. If it's too salty, add more rock sugar. Using tongs, remove the scallion whites, yellow onion, shallots, ginger, and spice pouch. Cover the broth and keep it warm over low heat.

8   To serve: Cook the phở noodles according to the package directions.

9   Divide the noodles among eight large bowls. Carefully remove the brisket and flank steak from the broth. Thinly slice the brisket and flank steak against the grain. Divide the meat among the bowls, making sure everyone gets some of each.

10 Arrange the scallion greens, cilantro, limes, mung bean sprouts, jalapeños, and pickled garlic on a plate so guests can add as much as they want to their soup. Ladle enough hot beef broth over the meat and noodles to cover. Each person can add more broth if they'd like more. Store any cooled leftover broth for up to 3 days in the fridge or freeze it for up to 1 month.

Here's the thing about being "that friend" who love

and events. If you're into having your friends and

your cheat sheet to being the most incredible dinner

I refer to the most when I want to impress my guest

are (when really, these dishes are simple to make!).

my bò kho birria or bring my

to cook: You end up hosting most of your own dinners

loved ones over as much as I do, this section will be

party host. These recipes are hits and the ones

Plus, they'll comment on how creative you

Switch up your typical Taco Tuesday with

xá xíu pulled pork sandwiches to your next barbecue—

they're like Fourth of July with a Vietnamese twist.

Entertaining

Sticky Ribs

Prep Time: *10 minutes*

Total Time: *40 minutes*

Makes *a first course for 2 or main course for 1*

3 tablespoons **oyster sauce**

2 tablespoons **honey**

1 tablespoon **soy sauce**

1 tablespoon **Chinkiang black vinegar**

1 teaspoon **sambal oelek**

½ pound **slab pork spare ribs**

¼ cup **cornstarch**

3 tablespoons **vegetable oil**

1 tablespoon **minced fresh ginger**

1 tablespoon **minced garlic**

1 **lime**, halved

½ teaspoon **sesame seeds**, toasted

2 **scallions**, thinly sliced on the diagonal

Steamed White Rice (page 26), for serving

Let's be real, who doesn't love sticky ribs? I can guarantee you, these ribs will be one of your favorite meals to make. It's one of those dishes that will have you licking your fingers clean of my mouthwatering, full-flavored sauce. For maximum satisfaction, serve these babies over a bed of freshly steamed rice.

1 In a small bowl, combine the oyster sauce, honey, soy sauce, black vinegar, and sambal. Mix together and set aside.

2 Slice the ribs into individual pieces and dredge them in a thin layer of cornstarch on all sides and tap off any excess.

3 Heat the vegetable oil in a skillet over medium-high heat until shimmering, about 2 minutes. Fry the ribs until they develop a lovely, browned crust on all sides, 3 to 4 minutes per side.

4 Using tongs, transfer the ribs to a plate. Add the ginger and garlic to the pan. Cook, stirring, until they start to turn golden, about 1 minute. Carefully pour in the sauce mixture. Squeeze ½ of the lime over it and let it bubble for 1 minute.

5 Reduce the heat to medium and return the ribs to the pan. Flip them occasionally for an additional 3 minutes, making sure they are coated in sauce. Move the ribs to a platter and garnish with the sesame seeds and scallions. Enjoy with piping hot steamed white rice.

Shrimp toast is a snack you could bring to a potluck and everyone will ask you to send them the recipe. These palm-size sandwiches are a party favorite, so I always double it. I prefer shokupan or Japanese milk bread over store-bought white bread because it's fluffy, buttery, and has a mild sweet taste that balances the shrimp flavor. Go the extra mile and cut the crusts off the bread to make it look like a fancy tea sandwich.

Shrimp Toast

Prep Time: *15 minutes*

Total Time: *45 minutes*

Makes *6 half sandwiches*

- ½ pound **medium white shrimp**, cleaned and minced into a paste
- 4 **garlic cloves**, minced
- 1 tablespoon **shallot**, minced
- 1 tablespoon **potato starch**
- 1 teaspoon **fish sauce**
- 1 teaspoon **garlic powder**
- 1 teaspoon **Old Bay Seasoning**
- 1 **large egg white**
- 6 slices **shokupan** (Japanese milk bread)
- **Avocado oil**, for shallow-frying (about 1½ cups)
- ½ cup **Sweet Chili Sauce** (page 185), for serving

1 In a small bowl, combine the shrimp paste, garlic, shallot, potato starch, fish sauce, garlic powder, Old Bay, and egg white. Mix it with a spatula.

2 Cut the crusts off the bread (or leave them on, if you prefer!). Spread ⅔ cup of the shrimp mixture onto one side of a slice of bread. Sandwich it together with another slice. Repeat with the 4 remaining slices of bread to make a total of 3 sandwiches.

3 Nest a wire rack in a sheet pan and place near the stove. Pour ½ inch of the avocado oil into a 10-inch skillet and heat over medium-high heat until it reaches 350°F. Working with one sandwich at a time, shallow-fry it until the bread is golden and the shrimp has turned to opaque pink, 2 to 3 minutes. Remove the sandwich from the oil, flip it onto a plate, and carefully slide it back into the oil. Cook the other side until the bread is golden brown, another 2 to 3 minutes. Drain the sandwich on the prepared wire rack. Repeat with the remaining sandwiches.

4 Slice the sandwiches in half on the diagonal and transfer to a platter. Enjoy with a side of sweet chili sauce in a small bowl.

Chicken and Ginger Dumplings

Prep Time: *30 minutes*
Total Time: *2 hours*
Makes *16 dumplings*

Making dumplings is the perfect way to spend some quality bonding time with your loved ones. You can certainly make them on your own, but it goes much faster with an assembly line of friends and family. You can buy premade dumpling wrappers or try your hand at making them yourself. Either way, no judgment! I prefer making the wrappers myself because the dough is softer and more forgiving. These little packages are garlicky, gingery, and have a pillowy soft, chewy texture. I have yet to meet a dumpling I didn't like, but these? I love.

FILLING:

- 1 pound **ground chicken**
- 6 **garlic cloves,** minced
- 2-inch knob **fresh ginger,** peeled and minced
- 3 **scallions,** thinly sliced
- 2 tablespoons **soy sauce**
- 1 tablespoon **oyster sauce**
- 1 tablespoon **sesame oil**
- 1 teaspoon **sugar**
- 1 teaspoon **cornstarch**
- 1 teaspoon **freshly ground black pepper**

DUMPLINGS:

- 2 cups **all-purpose flour,** plus more for dusting
- 1 cup **hot water**

DIPPING SAUCE:

- 2 tablespoons **soy sauce**
- 1 tablespoon **Lemongrass Chili Oil** (page 186)
- 1 tablespoon **Chinkiang black vinegar**

1   Make the filling: In a large bowl, combine the chicken, garlic, ginger, scallions, soy sauce, oyster sauce, sesame oil, sugar, cornstarch, and black pepper. Give it a good mix. Cover and refrigerate until ready to use.

2   Make the dumplings: In a heatproof bowl, use a spatula to combine the flour and hot water. Once the mixture cools down enough, use your hands to knead it into a sticky dough. Dust a clean kitchen surface with flour and knead the dough until you can roll it into a smooth ball, about 10 minutes. Cover it with a kitchen towel and let rest for 20 minutes.

3   Divide the dough into 4 equal portions. On a lightly floured surface, roll each portion into a thin log, then cut it into 4 pieces (about 1 ounce each). Lightly dust in flour and transfer to a baking sheet. Cover the dough with a kitchen towel to prevent it from drying out as you work. Take 1 piece of dough and roll it into a ball with your hands, then roll it out with a dusted rolling pin to make a round as flat as possible and 3 to 4 inches in diameter. Repeat with the rest of the dough pieces. Do not stack the wrappers or they might stick together.

4   Scoop 1 tablespoon of the filling and place it into the middle of a wrapper. (If you're using premade wrappers, dip a finger in a small bowl of water and run it around the edges.) Fold the dough in half over the filling to make a half-moon shape and pinch it closed. Get ready to practice your pleats: Starting at one point of the half-moon, pleat the edges and pinch as you work your way around the curve toward the other end. Repeat with the rest of the dough and filling.

5   Line a bamboo steamer basket with parchment paper. Arrange the dumplings in the basket ½ inch apart, keeping in mind that they will expand slightly.

6   Fill a large pot halfway with water and bring it to a vigorous boil over high heat, then reduce the heat to medium. Set the steamer over the pot and steam the dumplings until they are puffed up and no longer look raw, about 15 minutes. Remove from the heat and let rest covered for 5 minutes.

7   Meanwhile, make the dipping sauce: In a small bowl, mix together the soy sauce, lemongrass chili oil, and black vinegar.

8   Serve the dumplings from the steamer with a plate underneath or transfer the dumplings carefully to a platter. Set the bowl of dipping sauce alongside.

Grilled Scallops

Prep Time: *5 minutes*
Total Time: *25 minutes*
Makes *8 scallops*

I had so many unforgettable moments on my last trip to Vietnam, which I was able to share with not just my team, but two amazing groups of supporters. Together we immersed ourselves in the beauty and deliciousness of Vietnamese culture. We visited the Red Boat Fish Sauce barrel house in Phú Quốc, Vietnam. The founder and owner, Cuong Pham, and his daughters, Tiffany and Tracy, treated us to an amazing lunch that featured grilled scallops. It was such a noteworthy dish that I had to re-create it for you. Try to find fresh scallops in the shell because their shells double as a serving plate! But if you can only find cleaned scallops, use a dish that can hold all the cooking juices and withstand the high heat of the broiler or grill.

8 whole **in-shell scallops**

¼ cup **Scallion Oil** (page 177)

2 tablespoons **fish sauce**

2 teaspoons **sugar**

½ cup **roasted salted peanuts,** crushed

1 Shuck the scallops by sliding an oyster knife between the two shells and turning it like a key. Carefully slide the knife away from you and along the inside of the shell to dislodge it. Open it up and remove the frilly mantle (also known as the skirt) and black gut. The mantle can be used for fish stock but discard the black gut. Separate the white adductor muscle and crescent-shaped orange-pink roe from the

shell. Do not throw the curved bottom shell away because it will be your baking and serving vessel.

2 Preheat a grill to high. (Alternatively, preheat the oven to 450°F.)

3 In a small bowl, stir together the scallion oil, fish sauce, and sugar. Place each scallop and roe on a curved half shell. Drizzle 1 teaspoon of the scallion mixture over each of the scallops.

4 Grill until they bubble, about 5 minutes. Close the grill top and continue to grill for 2 minutes. (Alternatively, transfer the scallops to a baking sheet and roast until bubbling, about 5 minutes. Remove the scallops and change the oven setting to broil. Broil on the top rack for 2 minutes.)

5 Brush more of the scallion oil on each scallop and sprinkle with the crushed peanuts. Serve the scallop shells on a trivet or with a towel underneath; they will be hot.

Spicy Clam Curry

Prep Time: *10 minutes*

Total Time: *40 minutes*

Makes *a first course for 4 or main course for 2*

My spicy clam curry evolved from a dish I made on an episode of *Chopped*, a competition show on the Food Network where you must cook with mystery ingredients in a basket. In the first round, I got Japanese raindrop cake, baked feta, mussels, and microgreens. I used the feta in a tomato sauce, added the raindrop cake for some sweetness, and then tossed the mussels in it. I plated the whole thing with a simple microgreen salad and a slice of toasted bread. Even though my entry was a success, I thought it could be more cohesive if I'd had another chance to try again. After a few tweaks and changes to the flavor profile, I think I have a real winner in this clam curry. You can try using white clams, Manila clams, or any other shellfish you find at the grocery store.

1 pound **Manila clams**

1 cup **chicken stock** or **water**

8 tablespoons (4 ounces) **unsalted butter**

1 **white onion**, diced

1 **shallot**, minced

4 **garlic cloves**, minced

1 tablespoon **minced fresh ginger**

1 tablespoon **tomato paste**

2 tablespoons **chili powder**

1 tablespoon **ground coriander**

1 tablespoon **garam masala**

1 tablespoon **ground turmeric**

1 teaspoon **ground cloves**

1½ cups **canned coconut milk**

2 tablespoons **finely chopped fresh parsley leaves**

Steamed White Rice (page 26), sliced baguette, or crispy rice crackers, for serving

1 In a 10-inch sauté pan, combine the clams and chicken stock, cover, and set over medium-high heat. Cook until the clams open naturally, 4 to 5 minutes. Discard any that stay closed after 10 minutes. Transfer the cooked clams to a bowl. Reserve the leftover stock for another use.

2 In the same pan, melt the butter over medium-high heat. Add the white onion, shallot, garlic, and ginger and cook, stirring occasionally, until the onion is translucent, 5 to 7 minutes.

3 Stir in the tomato paste and reduce the heat to medium. Stir in the chili powder, coriander, garam masala, turmeric, and cloves and cook for 5 minutes.

4 Stir in the coconut milk and simmer for 1 minute. Add the clams to the pan and toss in the curry to coat. Remove from the heat.

5 Transfer the clam curry to a shallow bowl. Garnish with the parsley. Serve hot with steamed white rice, sliced baguette, or crispy rice crackers.

BBH Soup Dumplings

Prep Time: *1 hour 15 minutes*
Total Time: *12 hours*
Makes *120 soup dumplings*

DUMPLING DOUGH:

6 cups **all-purpose flour,** plus more for dusting

3 cups **hot water**

FILLING:

1 pound **ground pork**

½ pound **ground beef** (80/20)

3 **scallions,** finely chopped

1 tablespoon **Shaoxing wine**

1 tablespoon **Lemongrass Saté** (page 181)

1 tablespoon **soy sauce**

1 teaspoon **fish sauce**

½ teaspoon **ground white pepper**

½ teaspoon **sugar**

½ teaspoon **sesame oil**

1 heaping cup **BBH Broth Cubes** (recipe follows)

DIPPING SAUCE:

⅓ cup **soy sauce**

⅓ cup **Chinkiang black vinegar**

⅓ cup **Lemongrass Saté** (page 181)

Soup dumplings are so much fun to eat. Delicate dumpling wrappers house juicy meat and piping hot soup. How do you get soup into a dumpling? The secret is a highly fatty and gelatinous broth that you chill and cut into cubes. That way, they're easier to handle when folding the dumplings. I feel like they are the perfect blank canvas for experimenting with different kinds of broth. I wanted to pair the classic spicy taste of Bún Bò Huế (page 134) with the format of a soup dumpling.

If you've never had soup dumplings, here's how to eat them: With chopsticks, gently lift the knot onto your Chinese soup spoon (not a regular spoon!). Take a small bite of the dough to let some of the soup seep out onto the spoon and once you've given it a few moments to cool, you can sip the remaining juice out of the dumpling and then eat the rest of the skin! Resist consuming them in one bite because the inside is filled with scalding hot broth.

(recipe continues)

1   First, make the dumpling dough: Measure the all-purpose flour into a bowl. Carefully pour the hot water into the bowl while stirring the flour with a fork. Once the dough starts to come together and it is cool enough to handle, dump it out onto a lightly floured surface and knead until it reaches a soft, smooth texture, about 10 minutes. It should not be sticky. Cover with a towel and let rest at room temperature for 1 hour.

2   On a floured surface, divide the dough into 4 equal portions. Roll each portion into a log 1 inch thick. Divide each log into 30 pieces, weighing 12 grams each (like a piece of gnocchi!). Cover the dough pieces with a damp towel as you work to prevent them from drying out.

3   Make the filling: In a bowl, combine the ground pork, ground beef, scallions, Shaoxing wine, lemongrass saté, soy sauce, fish sauce, white pepper, sugar, and sesame oil. Mix it well with a spatula. Gently fold the BBH broth cubes into the meat, making sure it is evenly distributed. Cover lightly with plastic wrap and refrigerate until ready to use.

4   When ready to assemble and cook, roll each piece of dumpling dough into a smooth ball and remember to keep them covered with a towel as you work. Working with one at a time, roll out each dough ball on a floured surface into a flat disc as thin as you can without ripping it. Place 1 tablespoon of filling in the center. Make small pleats along the circumference of the dough disc and pinch it closed at the top. Repeat this step until you run out of dough pieces. If you are having a hard time closing the dumplings, reduce the filling to 2 teaspoons. You'll be able to stuff more filling in as you improve your pleats.

5   Line a two-tiered bamboo steamer basket with parchment paper. Working in batches, arrange the dumplings in the basket 1 inch apart.

6   Fill a large pot halfway with water and bring it to a vigorous boil over high heat, then reduce the heat to medium. Set the steamer over the pot and steam until the dumplings are no longer doughy and have relaxed against the filling, about 10 minutes. A dumpling should look like a small volcano. Repeat the steaming process with the rest of the dumplings, making sure to refill the water to halfway up the side of the pot.

7   Meanwhile, make the dipping sauce: In a small bowl, stir together the soy sauce, black vinegar, and lemongrass saté.

8   Serve the dumplings immediately from the steamer with a plate underneath. Set ramekins of the dipping sauce alongside.

BBH Broth Cubes

Prep Time: *15 minutes*

Total Time: *10 hours*

Makes *1 quart cubes*

4 **fresh lemongrass stalks**

2 tablespoons **vegetable oil,** plus more if needed

1 **shallot,** roughly chopped

3 **garlic cloves,** smashed and peeled

2 **fresh Thai bird's eye chilies,** thinly sliced

3 **unsmoked ham hocks**

2 pounds **beef bones,** rinsed with cold water

$\frac{1}{2}$ pound **pork skin**

$\frac{1}{2}$ cup **fresh pineapple chunks**

1 tablespoon **fish sauce,** plus more to taste

$\frac{1}{2}$ teaspoon **shrimp paste**

1   Remove the dry, outermost layer from each lemongrass stalk. Trim the top 5 inches and 1 inch from the bottom root end, leaving you with a tender white center. Bruise the stalks with a pestle, rolling pin, or bottom of a pot.

2   Heat the 2 tablespoons vegetable oil (or enough to coat the bottom of the pot) in a large pot over medium-high heat until shimmering, about 2 minutes. Add the lemongrass, shallot, garlic, and chilies and cook, stirring constantly, until slightly charred, about 2 minutes. Scoot the aromatics to the side and add the ham hocks. Give them a good sear on each side, 3 to 4 minutes per side.

3   Add the cleaned beef bones, pork skin, pineapple chunks, and enough water to submerge everything in the pot (about 6 cups). Use a wooden spoon to scrape up any aromatics that might have stuck to the bottom. Bring to a boil over high heat. Reduce the heat to low and simmer for 3 hours. Periodically skim off any scum that floats to the top.

4   Strain the broth into a large container, then stir in the fish sauce and shrimp paste. Taste and adjust the seasoning with more fish sauce, if needed. Cool the broth to room temperature for 1 hour.

5   Carefully pour the broth onto a quarter sheet pan or 9 × 13-inch baking dish. Cover and refrigerate for 6 hours or overnight to set the gelatin. Once the broth is set, discard any solidified fat from the top and cut the gelled broth into $\frac{1}{2}$-inch cubes. Refrigerate any you need that day until you use it. Freeze the rest of the broth for up to 1 month for future batches.

BBQ Duck Buns

Prep Time: *4 hours*

Total Time: *5 hours 25 minutes*

Makes *10 duck bao buns*

BAO BUNS:

¾ cup **whole milk**

2 teaspoons **sugar**

1 teaspoon **active dry yeast**

2 cups **all-purpose flour,** plus more for dusting

1 teaspoon **baking powder**

¼ teaspoon **kosher salt**

2 tablespoons **vegetable oil**, plus more for the bowl

BBQ DUCK:

4 **Peking** or **Long Island duck breasts** (6 ounces each)

2 tablespoons **sugar**

2 tablespoons **kosher salt**

2 tablespoons **five-spice powder**

¼ cup **honey**

2 tablespoons **Shaoxing wine**

2 tablespoons **apple cider vinegar**

1 tablespoon **oyster sauce**

1 tablespoon **soy sauce**

FOR SERVING:

4 thinly sliced **Persian (mini) cucumbers**

4 **scallions,** julienned and shocked in cold water

I've never met a plate of BBQ duck buns that I didn't like, so if you've never had them, this is your wake-up call! It's my favorite item to order when I get dim sum and the one thing I look forward to the most at Vietnamese weddings. If you know, you know. What's cool about making the steamed buns yourself is that you can freeze them for up to a month and resteam when you need them again. They'll retain their pillowy softness! Buns are a great medium for experimentation, too, so have fun trying it with my Crispy Pork Belly (page 56), Bò Lúc Lắc (page 32), or Honey-Glazed Shrimp (page 67). Don't skip out on the basting; it's crucial for caramelizing the glaze and rendering the duck fat.

1   Make the bao buns: In a large bowl, whisk together the milk, sugar, and yeast. Set it aside in a warm place for 10 minutes to bloom.

2   Sift the flour, baking powder, and salt into another large bowl. Pour the milk mixture into the dry ingredients and mix well with a spoon until the dough comes together.

(recipe continues)

3   Dust a work surface with flour and knead the dough by hand until the dough is smooth and no longer sticky, about 5 minutes. Form it into a ball and transfer it to an oiled bowl. Cover the dough with a damp towel and let it rise for 1 hour.

4   Meanwhile, cut out ten 3-inch squares of parchment paper.

5   After the 1-hour mark, punch down the dough and divide it into 10 equal portions. Keep the dough covered with a damp towel as you work. Take a portion of dough and roll it into a ball. With a dusted rolling pin, roll it out into an oval 4 inches long. Brush some of the vegetable oil on one side of the oval and fold it in half, the oiled sides touching each other. Repeat with the rest of the dough. Place each of the dough pieces on a square of parchment paper, set aside, and cover with a damp towel. Let rise for an additional 20 minutes.

6   Arrange the buns, on their parchment squares, in a 2-tier bamboo steamer. Make sure the paper squares do not touch.

7   In a large pot, bring 3 inches of water to a vigorous boil over high heat, then reduce the heat to medium. Set the steamer over the pot and steam the buns until puffed and soft to the touch, about 10 minutes. Remove from the heat and let sit covered for 10 minutes.

8   Make the BBQ duck: Score the skin of the duck breasts in a crosshatch pattern, making sure to not cut into the flesh. Pat the breasts dry with a paper towel. In a small bowl, stir together the sugar, salt, and five-spice powder. Coat each duck breast with the spice mixture, making sure to get into the crevices.

9   Place the duck breasts on a sheet pan and refrigerate, uncovered, for 1 to 2 hours to dry out (if you have the time, do this overnight!). When they're ready to cook, take the duck breasts out and bring to room temperature for 30 minutes.

10   Preheat the oven to 450°F.

11   In a small bowl, whisk together the honey, Shaoxing wine, vinegar, oyster sauce, and soy sauce. Set the glaze near the stovetop.

12   Place the duck breasts skin-side down in a cold ovenproof skillet (preferably cast iron) and set the pan over high heat. Let the skin crisp up slowly, 4 to 6 minutes. Using tongs, turn them over to sear for an additional 2 minutes.

13   Take the duck breasts off the heat and place on a baking sheet skin-side up, brush the glaze on the skin, and place it in the oven for 5 minutes. Repeat this basting step two more times until the skin has crisped up and the duck reaches an internal temperature of 165°F.

14   To serve: Thinly slice the duck breasts. Transfer to a platter with the warm bao buns, cucumbers, drained scallion curls, and a small bowl of hoisin sauce.

Tamarind Crab Legs

Cua Rang Me

Cua rang me is stir-fried tamarind crab, a popular entree in Vietnam. The crab is typically served whole, which is visually impressive, with a signature sweet and sour tamarind sauce covering the whole shell. The only thing I don't enjoy (you know I love crab!) about the dish is how difficult it is to eat. I solved this problem by using king crab legs and splitting them, making it much easier to get at the meat.

Prep Time: *10 minutes*
Total Time: *35 minutes*
Makes *a main course for 2*

- ½ cup **seedless tamarind paste**, torn into small pieces
- ½ cup **water**
- 6 tablespoons **fish sauce**
- ¼ cup **light brown sugar**
- 2 tablespoons **oyster sauce**
- 2 teaspoons **tomato paste**
- **Avocado oil**, for frying (about 2 cups)
- 8 **king crab legs**
- 1 cup **cornstarch**
- 1 tablespoon **minced garlic**
- ¼ cup **roasted unsalted peanuts** (optional), crushed

1 In a small pan, stir together the tamarind paste and water over medium-low heat until completely liquefied, about 2 minutes. Strain the tamarind paste through a fine-mesh sieve into a bowl. Whisk in the fish sauce, brown sugar, oyster sauce, and tomato paste. Set the tamarind mixture aside.

2 Nest a wire rack in a sheet pan and set near the stove. Pour ½ inch avocado oil into a large pot over medium-high heat until a wooden chopstick bubbles when you insert it.

3 Cut the crab legs into 4-inch-long pieces and split in half lengthwise with a sharp knife or with kitchen scissors. Lightly coat the crab legs in the cornstarch and tap off any excess starch. Working in two batches, carefully fry the crab legs in the oil until they turn a nice golden color and the shells have turned bright orange, about 2 minutes. Transfer the fried legs to the wire rack. Repeat with the other half of the legs.

4 Heat 2 tablespoons avocado oil in a skillet over medium-high heat until shimmering, about 2 minutes. Add the garlic and tamarind mixture and cook, stirring. until bubbling, about 1 minute. Toss the fried crab legs in the sauce, making sure that every piece is coated!

5 Transfer the crab legs to a platter. Pour any sauce left in the pan over the crab. If desired, garnish with the peanuts.

Xá Xíu Pulled Pork Sandwiches

Prep Time: *7 hours 40 minutes*
Total Time: *15 hours 25 minutes*
Makes *8 sandwiches*

Pulled pork is a quintessential American BBQ staple and there's a reason: It's delicious. I asked myself, "What would a pulled pork sandwich look like if it was Asian?" I credit my Filipino friends for introducing me to the magic that is Jufran Banana Sauce, which is essentially banana ketchup. You read that right! It changes the condiment game, especially for people who want a sweeter, less vinegary alternative to regular ketchup. I'll admit, this recipe is time-consuming, but it's worth it, especially if you're having people over for a game night. Switch the brioche out for slider buns, secure with a toothpick, and you've got yourself a party.

PULLED PORK:

4- to 6-pound **bone-in, skin-on pork shoulder**

½ cup (packed) **dark brown sugar**

3 tablespoons **oyster sauce**

3 tablespoons **soy sauce**

2 tablespoons **hoisin sauce**

2 tablespoons **garlic salt**

2 tablespoons **Shaoxing wine**

2 tablespoons **five-spice powder**

1 tablespoon **onion powder**

SAUCE:

3 tablespoons **honey**

2 tablespoons **apple cider vinegar**

½ cup **Jufran banana sauce**

SLAW:

1 cup (packed) **shredded red cabbage**

1 cup (packed) **shredded green cabbage**

1 cup shredded peeled **carrot**

1 cup **shredded jicama**

¾ cup **Kewpie mayonnaise**

3 tablespoons **fresh lime juice**

Kosher salt and **freshly ground black pepper**

SANDWICHES:

8 **brioche buns**, split horizontally

1 cup **Dưa Chua** (page 193), thinly sliced

(recipe continues)

1   Make the pulled pork: Use a fork and stab the pork slab all over so the marinade can really seep in. Once you've gotten your anger out, make the marinade.

2   In a medium bowl, combine the brown sugar, oyster sauce, soy sauce, hoisin sauce, garlic salt, Shaoxing wine, five-spice powder, and onion powder. Whisk it together. Pour the marinade into a gallon zipper bag or one that can fit the whole piece of pork. Place the pork in the bag with the marinade. Seal it and give it a nice massage. Place the bag on a sheet pan and refrigerate for a good 6 hours or overnight, the longer the better. Once it's ready, take the pork out of the fridge and let it come to room temperature for 1 hour.

3   Preheat the oven to 250°F.

4   Nest a wire rack in a sheet pan. Remove the pork from the bag and place it on the rack. Reserve the marinade for the sauce.

5   Fill a deep baking pan halfway with water and place it on the lowest rack in the oven. Set the marinated pork on the rack above it and slow-cook for 7 hours. Check the water pan and refill every couple of hours to make sure it has not evaporated.

6   Remove the pork from the oven and let it rest for 20 minutes. Discard the water in the other pan. Once the pork is cool enough to handle, shred the meat with two forks and discard the bones. Cover the meat with a piece of foil and store in the still-warm oven until you're ready to eat.

7   Make the sauce: In a small saucepan, combine the honey, vinegar, banana sauce, and the reserved marinade. Stir the sauce mixture over medium heat until it comes to a boil and becomes a nice thick sauce, 6 to 8 minutes. Set aside to cool.

8   Make the slaw: In a large bowl, toss together the red and green cabbages, the carrot, and jicama. Add the mayonnaise and lime juice and toss again. Adjust the seasoning with salt and pepper to your liking.

9   Assemble the sandwiches: Toast the brioche buns. For each sandwich, slather the sauce on the bottom bun and add 1 cup of the shredded pork on top. Add another generous slather of the sauce. Pile on $\frac{1}{4}$ cup of slaw, 2 tablespoons of dưa chua, and the top bun. Serve on a large platter.

Bò Kho "Birria" Tacos

Over the past decade, birria tacos have taken the international food landscape by storm. They hail from Jalisco, Mexico, but now you can find them at food trucks and fancy restaurants across the United States. Here in Los Angeles, you can't go a block without running into a truck or taco spot. Birria is an amazing slow-cooked beef stew with lots of spices and chilies. A tortilla is soaked in its rich consommé, fried with melty cheese, and filled with super-tender beef. It's then served with its flavorful broth on the side. Birria is like a Mexican version of a French dip sandwich, but even better. The whole process reminds me of bò kho, a spicy Vietnamese beef stew. I wanted to expand this Mexican concept with Vietnamese flavors. Corn is a staple in Mexico and I pay tribute to it by using corn tortillas over flour. I guarantee you'll want to make multiple batches, because who can really eat just one taco, right?

Prep Time: *40 minutes*
Total Time: *4 hours 40 minutes*
Makes *6 tacos*

2 **fresh lemongrass stalks**

1 pound **beef stew meat**

2 tablespoons **minced garlic**

2 tablespoons **minced shallots**

2 tablespoons **fish sauce**

1 tablespoon **oyster sauce**

1 tablespoon **dark soy sauce**

1 tablespoon **light brown sugar**

1 tablespoon **five-spice powder**

2 tablespoons **vegetable oil**

3 whole **star anise**

2-inch knob **fresh ginger,** peeled and sliced into planks

2 to 3 **dried red chilies,** to taste

2 tablespoons **tomato paste**

4 to 5 cups **beef stock**

1 **cinnamon stick**

6 (6-inch) **corn tortillas**

¾ cup **shredded mozzarella** or **Oaxaca cheese**

1 **white onion,** finely diced

4 sprigs **fresh cilantro,** stems removed

2 **limes,** cut into wedges

(recipe continues)

1   Remove the dry, outermost layer from each lemongrass stalk. Trim the top 5 inches and 1 inch from the bottom root end, leaving you with a tender white center. Bruise the stalks with a pestle, rolling pin, or bottom of a pot. Mince one of the stalks and set the whole stalk aside.

2   In a medium bowl, stir together the beef, minced lemongrass, 1 tablespoon of the garlic, 1 tablespoon of the shallot, the fish sauce, oyster sauce, dark soy sauce, brown sugar, and five-spice powder. Make sure the beef is fully coated. Cover and marinate for 30 minutes at room temperature or longer in the fridge (as I always say: the longer, the better).

3   Heat the vegetable oil in a large pot over medium-high heat until shimmering, about 1 minute. Brown the beef, 2 to 3 minutes on each side. Using tongs, transfer the meat to a plate.

4   Add the star anise, ginger, chilies, tomato paste, the remaining 1 tablespoon garlic, and remaining 1 tablespoon shallot to the pot. Cook, stirring, for 1 minute to combine. Return the meat to the pot along with 3 cups of the beef stock, making sure to scrape up the flavorful bits on the bottom of the pot. Add the cinnamon stick and the remaining lemongrass stalk and bring to a boil over high heat. Reduce to a slow simmer over medium-low heat, cover, and cook for 1 hour.

5   Add 1 to 2 cups more beef stock to ensure that the meat is covered and continue cooking until the meat starts to fall apart. It should take about 2 hours more and once it reaches that stage you are ALMOST done (lol).

6   Using tongs, carefully remove the meat to a sheet pan and shred it with two forks. Keep the sauce warm over low heat. Pour a ladle's worth of sauce over the shredded beef and cover it with a lid or piece of foil to keep it moist.

7   Dip both sides of a tortilla into the warm sauce and set it in a skillet over medium heat. To the tortilla, add $\frac{1}{3}$ cup of shredded meat, 2 tablespoons of the mozzarella, 1 tablespoon of the onion, and a few leaves of cilantro. Fold it in half (like a taco, duh!).

8   Give it a few flips in the pan until the broth has been absorbed into the tortilla and the cheese melts, 1 to 2 minutes. It's okay if some cheese spills out and crisps.

9   Transfer the taco to a platter. Repeat with the remaining tacos. Squeeze a few lime wedges over the tacos. Serve with more lime wedges on the side.

This sweet and sour roasted fish is unlike any other dish in this collection. Another Vietnamese fish dish, cá sốt cà chua, inspired my take. The fish is typically deep-fried whole and covered in a tomato-based sauce. Picture my version: a tangy sweet and sour sauce atop crunchy skin and delicate fish flesh. Instead of frying, I opt to roast the fish to bring out more of its deep flavor. I've experimented with many varieties of fish, but those that stood out were branzino, halibut, and snapper. Don't skimp on cleaning your fish! When I say clean, I mean gutted, scaled, and washed in its entirety. Some fishmongers will help you most of the way, but it's best to be sure and learn to do it yourself.

Sweet and Sour Roasted Fish

Prep Time: *10 minutes*
Total Time: *40 minutes*
Makes *1 whole fish for 4*

1 **whole fish** (2 to 3 pounds), cleaned

Olive oil

1 teaspoon **kosher salt**

1 teaspoon **freshly ground black pepper**

5 **garlic cloves,** smashed and peeled

1 **lemon,** thinly sliced

1 cup **Sweet Chili Sauce** (page 185)

1 Position racks in the middle and top third of the oven and preheat the oven to 425°F.

2 With the fish sitting horizontally on the cutting board in front of you, score 3 vertical slashes on the fish. Flip it over and repeat on the other side. Oil the cavity and outside of the fish. Season with the salt and pepper in the cavity and on the skin of the fish. Place the garlic and lemon in the cavity.

3 Transfer the fish to a wire rack nested in a sheet pan. Transfer to the middle rack of the oven and roast until the flesh is opaque white and some juices have gathered on the pan below it, about 10 minutes.

4 Flip the fish carefully with a spatula and roast for another 10 minutes. Remove the pan from the oven. Switch the oven to broil. Broil the fish on the top rack for 1 minute on each side.

5 With a long fish spatula, transfer the fish to a platter and pour the sweet chili sauce on top.

This is for all the sauce lovers out there! Sauces and that ties it all together. It's important to master your needs that "extra something." Of course, this collection specifically in Vietnam. Fish sauce is a prominent it's important to pay attention to its measurements; a balance of an entire dish. The following pages will chili sauce, peanut sauce, and lemongrass chili oil

sauces   and

condiments are the final, unifying part of a dish

sauces so you can always rely on them when your food

is centered around Asian flavors and atmosphere,

ingredient in a variety of East Asian cuisines, but

little too much or too little can throw off the

have everything you need to make your own sweet

stock your fridge regularly or you'll run out quickly.

condiments

Nước mắm is the most iconic dipping sauce in Vietnam, but every family makes it differently. Though it has many variations, at its core it's an incredibly simple sauce to make. When you hit that perfect salt/umami/sweet spot, it really helps bring your dishes to new heights. Traditionally, nước mắm is made with anchovies, sea salt, and water, but for our convenience, any bottled fish sauce will do the trick.

Sweet Fish Sauce

Nước Mắm

Prep Time: *15 minutes*
Total Time: *20 minutes*
Makes *1½ cups*

- 3 tablespoons plus 1½ teaspoons **sugar**
- 3 tablespoons **fish sauce**
- 2 tablespoons **distilled white vinegar**
- 2 teaspoons **sambal oelek**
- 1 cup **hot water**
- 3 **garlic cloves,** minced
- 2 **fresh Thai bird's eye chilies,** minced

1 In a heatproof bowl, whisk together the sugar, fish sauce, vinegar, sambal, and hot water. Let the mixture cool down in the fridge for 10 minutes.

2 Stir the garlic and chilies into the chilled mixture.

3 Transfer the nước mắm to a plastic container and store covered in the fridge for up to 2 weeks.

Ginger Fish Sauce

Nước Mắm Gừng

Prep Time: *5 minutes*
Total Time: *10 minutes*
Makes *2 cups*

I think by this point in the book, you can tell how much I love sauces that can work with many dishes. My ginger fish sauce is no exception. I typically serve it with Cháo Gà (page 102) and Gỏi Gà (page 107), but you can also douse it on grilled shrimp or raw oysters. Why is it so good? It's a perfect combination of sweet, sour, and spicy. Plus, you can customize it by increasing any one of its ingredients to highlight it. If you want it extra spicy, double the Thai bird's eye chili, or if you need a sweeter note, add more sugar.

5 tablespoons **fish sauce**

5 tablespoons **sugar**

1 cup **hot water**

Juice of 1 **lime**

2-inch knob **fresh ginger**, peeled and minced

1 **fresh Thai bird's eye chili** (optional), minced

1 In a small bowl, whisk together the fish sauce, sugar, hot water, and lime juice until the sugar is dissolved. Stir in the ginger and Thai bird's eye chili (if using). Taste and adjust the seasoning with either more sugar or lime juice.

2 Store covered in a plastic container in the fridge for up to 2 weeks (but honestly, it never lasts that long).

Scallion Oil

Scallion oil is a simple condiment that you can use to add a burst of oniony flavor to any dish. It also adds a mouthwatering gloss to meats and vegetables. It's so easy to make that it won't break any dish in this book, but will definitely make it. Try it on my Cơm Tấm (page 53), Grilled Scallops (page 150), or Bánh Bột Lọc (page 62). Want to know a secret? Save the oil from making Fried Shallots (page 194) and use it here to give your scallion oil a deeper allium flavor.

Prep Time: *5 minutes*
Total Time: *30 minutes*
Makes *1 cup*

1 cup **vegetable oil**

8 **scallions**, thinly sliced

¼ teaspoon **kosher salt**

1   In a small saucepan, heat the vegetable oil over high heat until you see it swirling slightly, about 5 minutes. Add the scallions to the oil and fry until they sizzle and turn a brighter shade of green, 1 to 2 minutes.

2   Take the pan off the heat and carefully transfer the scallion oil to a heatproof container. Stir in the salt and let it completely cool.

3   Cover and refrigerate for up to 1 week.

Bomb–Ass Ranch

Prep Time: *10 minutes*

Total Time: *15 minutes*

Makes *1½ cups*

One of my great joys in life is finding out a restaurant makes its own ranch dressing. Look, I think ranch can be complex. They can exist in a range, diversified in formula but still hold that original creamy/tangy/slightly herbaceous base flavor we all know and love. My bomb-ass ranch will deliver extra tang with the addition of apple cider vinegar. It works so well with my Tamarind Chicken Tenders (page 92) and as a dip for crudités. I thoroughly believe making ranch yourself will always be better than anything you buy in a bottle.

- ½ cup **buttermilk**
- ½ cup **sour cream**
- ½ cup **Kewpie mayonnaise**
- 1 tablespoon **finely chopped fresh chives**
- 1 tablespoon **finely chopped fresh dill**
- ½ teaspoon **Worcestershire sauce**
- ½ teaspoon **fish sauce**
- ½ teaspoon **apple cider vinegar**
- ½ teaspoon **onion powder**
- ½ teaspoon **garlic powder**

In a medium bowl, whisk together the buttermilk, sour cream, mayonnaise, chives, dill, Worcestershire sauce, fish sauce, vinegar, onion powder, and garlic powder until combined. Store in an airtight container in the fridge for up to 1 week.

Peanut sauce is served as a dip with my Chả Giò (page 60) and is also served as a typical condiment for chicken satay skewers or tossed with plain noodles. While various types of peanut sauce exist across Asia, mine has hoisin sauce for umami and sambal oelek for extra spice. You can choose the peanut butter texture of your choice, smooth or chunky, they're equally delicious.

Peanut Sauce

Prep Time: *15 minutes*
Total Time: *20 minutes*
Makes *1¼ cups*

1 tablespoon **canola oil**

5 **garlic cloves,** minced

1 cup **coconut milk** or **water**

5 tablespoons **hoisin sauce**

3 heaping tablespoons **chunky peanut butter**

1 tablespoon **sambal oelek**

¼ cup **roasted unsalted peanuts,** crushed

1   Heat the canola oil in a saucepan over medium heat until shimmering, about 1 minute. Add the garlic and cook, stirring, until it is golden, 1 to 2 minutes.

2   Stir in the coconut milk, hoisin sauce, and peanut butter. Bring the mixture to a boil while stirring, then remove from the heat and add the sambal. Give it a thorough mix.

3   Transfer the sauce to a heatproof container and let cool completely. Top the sauce off with the crushed peanuts. Cover and store for up to 1 week.

Lemongrass saté is the definition of versatility. While it sounds the same as Southeast Asian satay or sate grilled skewers, it is not the same thing! This unique Vietnamese condiment can be used as a marinade, a base for Bún Bò Huế (page 134), a finishing sauce, and a flavoring for stir-fries. The garlicky, spicy flavor of saté is the essence of Southeast Asian flavors and will undoubtedly become a staple in your kitchen. I recommend that as you make it, you blend each aromatic individually, one at a time, so they're evenly sized. That way, no one flavor overpowers the rest.

Lemongrass Saté

Prep Time: 20 minutes
Total Time: 50 minutes
Makes 1½ cups

6 **fresh lemongrass stalks**

6 **fresh Fresno chilies**, roughly chopped

4 **fresh Thai bird's eye chilies**, roughly chopped

10 **garlic cloves**, roughly chopped

1 **medium shallot**, roughly chopped

1 cup **avocado oil**

1 teaspoon **sugar**

1 teaspoon **fish sauce**

1 teaspoon **chicken bouillon powder**

1 Remove the dry, outermost layer from each lemongrass stalk. Trim the top 5 inches and 1 inch from the bottom root end, leaving you with a tender white center. Bruise the stalks.

2 Working with one ingredient at a time, in a blender or food processor, blend the lemongrass, Fresno chilies, Thai bird's eye chilies, garlic, and shallot, adding each to a medium saucepan as you work.

3 Add the avocado oil to the saucepan and cook over high heat until the oil starts to bubble, about 3 minutes. Stir in the sugar, fish sauce, and chicken bouillon powder. Make sure to scrape up any bits that stick to the bottom of the pan. Keep cooking the mixture over high heat, stirring occasionally, until the garlic turns golden brown, about 5 minutes. Reduce the heat to low and cook until the saté has thickened slightly, about 10 minutes.

4 Transfer the saté to a heatproof container and cool completely. Cover and store it in the fridge for up to 2 weeks.

Coconut Sauce

Prep Time: *20 minutes*

Total Time: *30 minutes*

Makes *1 pint*

Commonly referred to as the "Asian whipped cream" on FoodTok, coconut sauce is primarily used as a topping for desserts across many different cuisines. You'll see it in action on my Chè Ba Màu (page 214) and Chối Chiên (page 206). One of the best things about this sauce is it can be served warm, cold, or at room temperature, depending on the dessert you are dressing. It's a super-simple recipe that uses pantry staples you probably already have in your kitchen.

1 (13.5-ounce) **can coconut milk**

½ teaspoon **cornstarch**

3 tablespoons **sugar**

1   Warm up the coconut milk in a small saucepan over medium heat. Whisk in the sugar and cornstarch until the sugar has dissolved completely and the sauce has thickened, about 6 minutes. It should be pourable but still have body to it. Remove the pan from the heat and transfer the sauce to a heatproof container. Let cool for at least 15 minutes.

2   Cover and refrigerate for up to 1 week.

I'm a big fan of BBQ sauce, but I always gravitate toward tangy over sweet. Here I wanted to introduce the tanginess of tamarind to a sticky sweet BBQ sauce. Slather my tamarind BBQ sauce onto everything, from salmon to chicken wings, chicken tenders, crab, fries, pizza, and burritos. It's the perfect summertime flavor for when you're ready to throw down on the grill.

Tamarind BBQ Sauce

Prep Time: *35 minutes*
Total Time: *1 hour 5 minutes*
Makes *1 quart*

- 1 cup **seedless tamarind paste**, torn into pieces
- 1 tablespoon **vegetable oil**
- 1 small **yellow onion**, diced
- 4 **garlic cloves**, minced
- 1 cup **ketchup**
- 1 cup (packed) **light brown sugar**
- ½ cup **apple cider vinegar**
- ⅓ cup **soy sauce**
- ¼ cup **molasses**
- 2 tablespoons **honey**
- 1½ teaspoons **onion powder**
- 1½ teaspoons **garlic powder**
- 8 tablespoons (4 ounces) **unsalted butter**

1 In a small pot, combine the tamarind paste and 1 cup water. Bring to a boil over medium-high heat so the tamarind can loosen up, about 3 minutes. Stir the tamarind pulp until it is liquefied and strain it through a fine-mesh sieve into a heatproof bowl. Set aside to cool.

2 Heat the vegetable oil in a medium pot over medium heat. Add the onion and cook, stirring occasionally, until it turns a nice golden brown, about 5 minutes. Add the garlic and give it another stir. Pour in the strained tamarind, the ketchup, brown sugar, vinegar, soy sauce, molasses, honey, onion powder, and garlic powder. Give everything a quick whisk and simmer over medium-low heat, stirring occasionally, until thickened into a shiny dark sauce, about 10 minutes.

3 Remove from the heat. Whisk in the butter until it is completely melted.

4 Carefully transfer the sauce to a blender and mix slowly at low speed, then ramp it up to higher speed until it is smooth.

5 Transfer to a heatproof container and let cool for 30 minutes. Cover and store for up to 2 weeks.

When you think of sweet chili sauce, you probably think about the distinct bright red sauce in a glass bottle from the popular Thai brand, Mae Ploy. If you're unfamiliar with this versatile condiment, I promise your life will be forever changed. Sweet chili sauce has a wide range of uses, from dipping sauce for Chả Giò (page 60) to a marinade and a finishing sauce for my Sweet and Sour Roasted Fish (page 169). My version is fresher and brighter on account of the Fresno chilies. This sauce is a staple in my house, and I rarely go without having this stocked in my fridge!

Sweet Chili Sauce

Prep Time: *2 hours 10 minutes*
Total Time: *2 hours 35 minutes*
Makes *1½ cups*

5 **fresh Fresno chilies**, roughly chopped

1 to 2 **fresh Thai bird's eye chilies**, to taste, roughly chopped

8 **garlic cloves**, roughly chopped

1 cup **sugar**

½ cup **distilled white vinegar**

1 tablespoon **cornstarch**

1   In a food processor or blender, pulse the Fresno chilies, Thai bird's eye chilies, and garlic until everything is broken into small pieces. Be careful not to breathe in the pepper fumes when you open the lid.

2   In a saucepan, stir together the chili/garlic mixture, the sugar, and vinegar. Bring to a simmer over low heat and cook for 5 minutes.

3   In a small bowl, stir 3 tablespoons water into the cornstarch to make a slurry. Stir it into the chili sauce. Increase the heat to medium-high and bring to a boil. As soon as the sauce boils, remove from the heat.

4   Stir the sauce once more. Carefully transfer it to a heatproof container and refrigerate uncovered for at least 2 hours. Don't consume the sauce while it is still hot!

5   After it's been cooled completely, cover, and store for up to 2 weeks.

Lemongrass Chili Oil

Prep Time: *1 hour 10 minutes*

Total Time: *1 hour 30 minutes*

Makes *3 cups*

Once I started to get the hang of cooking with lemongrass, which was way easier than I thought it would be, I began trying to incorporate its flavor into different kinds of dishes and sauces. I dreamed of making Lemongrass Chili Oil Noodles (page 80), but I first had to figure out how to make the base: the chili oil itself. It's a spicy condiment that adds the perfect flavorful zing to any meal. At the beginning of the Covid-19 pandemic, everyone on TikTok was crazy for chili oil. I tried a few, most of them were just spicy oil, but the ones that stood out were soooo addicting. I wanted to make one with spicy depth, unique lemongrass flavor, and a craveable umami crunch.

I served this at my first ever Chị Hai pop-up and some people "accidentally" took a jar home because it was just that good. I can guarantee that once you have this stocked in your fridge, you'll use it as a topping for every meal you have. Spoon it over rice bowls, fried eggs, stir-fries, noodle soups, or add it to a dumpling dipping sauce. You really can't go wrong with it!

4 **fresh lemongrass stalks**

8 **garlic cloves**, roughly chopped

2 cups **avocado oil**

4 **dried red chilies**

3 whole **star anise**

2 tablespoons **sesame seeds**

1 **cinnamon stick**

½ cup **Fried Shallots** (page 194)

5 tablespoons **red pepper flakes**

4 **fresh Thai bird's eye chilies**, chopped

¼ cup **soy sauce**

4 teaspoons **sugar**

2 teaspoons **chicken bouillon powder**

1   Remove the dry, outermost layer from each lemongrass stalk. Trim the top 5 inches and 1 inch from the bottom root end, leaving you with a tender white center. Bruise the stalks with a pestle, rolling pin, or bottom of a pot. Roughly chop the stalks.

2   In a food processor, combine the lemongrass and garlic and pulse until they are minced. Scrape down the sides with a spatula and drizzle in up to 2 tablespoons of the avocado oil to help break it up.

3   In a 2-quart pot, heat the remaining avocado oil over medium heat until it reaches 200°F, about 5 minutes.

4   In a dry skillet, toast the dried red chilies, star anise, sesame seeds, and cinnamon over medium heat for 3 to 4 minutes to release the oils and flavor.

5   In a heatproof bowl, combine the chopped lemongrass/garlic mixture, toasted spices, fried shallots, pepper flakes, Thai bird's eye chilies, soy sauce, sugar, and chicken bouillon powder. Carefully pour the hot oil into the bowl and give it a mix so everything is combined. Let the lemongrass oil cool for 1 hour.

6   Transfer to an airtight container and store in the fridge for up to 2 weeks.

Pickled Daikon
and Carrots

Đồ Chua

Prep Time: *40 minutes*

Total Time: *1 hour*

Makes *1 pint*

If you've ever had Vietnamese food, you've probably had đồ chua before. These colorful Vietnamese pickles are served with just about everything, from bánh mì to rice plates, and Bánh Xèo (page 50). Compared to cucumber pickles, this magical combination of carrot and daikon radish is sweeter, crunchier, and more fun.

Depending on the size of your jars, you might have leftover pickle brine. Don't waste it! You can use it to pickle a small red onion, too. Add a teaspoon of kosher salt per leftover cup and whisk until it is dissolved. Simply julienne the onion and proceed with the final step of this recipe.

PICKLE BRINE:

1 cup **hot water**

1 cup **distilled white vinegar**

½ cup **sugar**

VEGETABLES:

2 tablespoons **kosher salt**

1 cup **carrot**, peeled and julienned

1 cup **daikon radish**, peeled and julienned

1   Make the pickle brine: In a large bowl, whisk together the hot water, vinegar, and sugar until the sugar dissolves.

2   Prepare the vegetables: In a medium bowl, sprinkle the salt over the carrots and daikon. Let it sit until the vegetables are flexible, 5 to 10 minutes. They should not break or snap when you bend them.

3   Rinse the salt from the vegetables, drain in a colander, and transfer to a jar or plastic container with a lid. Add the brine to the jar of vegetables. Cover it and refrigerate for 30 minutes.

4   It is ready to serve or can be kept covered in the fridge for up to 2 weeks.

Pickled Mustard Greens

Dưa Chua

Prep Time: *12 hour 35 minutes*

Total Time: *1 to 3 days*

Makes *2 quarts*

Dưa chua is a popular Vietnamese side dish that can be served with any meal of the day. Its distinct tangy flavor balances saltier or braised dishes such as Thịt Kho (page 42). Not to mention its addicting crunchy texture, which I highlight in Xá Xíu Pulled Pork (page 162). Depending on the warmth of your home and weather, the fermentation time might differ, but in hotter months the fermentation process should be done by the third day. I recommend leaving the jar in direct sunlight to cure the mustard greens faster. Taste it every day and once you've achieved your desired sourness, you can store the container in your fridge. Dưa chua will continue to ferment slowly in the fridge, but I'm sure you can finish your container within a week!

1   Break apart the mustard greens and clean in between the leaves with cold water. Cut the mustard greens into 1-inch bite-size pieces.

2   In a large bowl, toss together the mustard greens, onion, and 3 tablespoons of the salt. Let sit for 30 minutes. Wash off the salt and drain the vegetables very well.

3   In a large pot, combine 5 cups water, the sugar, vinegar, and remaining 3 tablespoons salt. Bring to a boil over high heat. Whisk until the sugar is dissolved. Remove from the heat and let it cool completely for 1 hour.

4   Divide the mustard greens and onion between two sterilized 1-quart jars. Add the cooled pickling liquid, cover, and let it sit in a warm place for at least 24 hours and up to 3 days. Once a day, open the jars to let out any gas that builds up. Taste the mustard greens each day and when you're happy with the flavor, store the jars in the fridge for up to 1 month.

2 pounds **Asian mustard greens**

1 medium **yellow onion**, julienned

6 tablespoons **kosher salt**

1 cup **sugar**

½ cup **distilled white vinegar**

Fried Shallots

Prep Time: *10 minutes*

Total Time: *25 minutes*

Makes *3 cups*

Fried shallots add a little sweet, aromatic crunch to any dish, whether it's salad, noodles, or a midday egg and rice bowl. Once you learn how to master this, I'm positive you're going to want them on everything. Shallots are incredibly versatile and milder in taste than onions, so I never have to worry about them overpowering other flavors. They're a great way to build flavor and crisply finish a dish. The trick is to slice the shallots as thin as possible with a mandoline or a sharp knife. Don't leave them in the oil unattended, they can burn quickly.

1   Slice the shallots into thin rings. Separate them as best as you can without breaking the rings.

2   Pour 2 inches canola oil into a medium pot or large deep saucepan and heat over medium-high heat until it reaches 350°F. Dip a wooden chopstick to test if it's ready, it should bubble.

3   Line a large plate with paper towels. Carefully add half of the sliced shallots to the hot oil. The oil may bubble up but will subside. Fry the shallots watching for hints of browning, about 5 minutes. Stir them a bit to keep the mixture

4 **large shallots,** peeled

Canola oil, for deep frying (about 1 quart)

moving for another 1 to 2 minutes. When most of the shallots are golden brown, remove with a slotted spoon or frying spider to the paper towels to drain. It's okay if a few strands are not quite brown yet, they will continue to cook slightly as they cool down.

4   Skim the oil with a slotted spoon to remove any burnt pieces and discard. Repeat the process with the remaining shallots, making sure to bring the oil back up to temperature.

5   Once drained and fully cooled, break up any strands that are clumped together. Transfer to a plastic container lined with a folded-up paper towel. Cover and store at room temperature for up to 1 week. Reserve the fragrant shallot oil for Scallion Oil (page 177) or everyday use.

If you've got a sweet tooth like me, you know no meal [is] respectfully, only-way to top off a savory meal is with a[...] guarantee your taste buds get the best of both worlds. [...] that I grew up eating in Vietnam and some that I've com[...] rarely allow me to order dessert at restaurants becaus[e...] dessert that catches my eye. I'm al[...] own versions and make them rea[...] cinnamon rolls, umami chocolat[...] the easiest fru[...]

D e S S

ever complete without dessert. The best—and,

qually refreshing and pleasant, sweet treat to

or this chapter, I wanted to include both desserts

p with on my own. When I was younger, my parents would

was too pricey. Now, I'm able to splurge on every

a point in my career where I can conceptualize my

n my kitchen. Don't miss my love letter to pandan in

hip cookies with a surprise ingredient, and chè Thái,

lad you'll ever make.

erts

Egg coffee is made by beating an egg yolk with condensed milk. It takes on a light, airy texture that you can use as a topping for coffee. Think "cold foam" but richer and silkier. I didn't know what to think about egg coffee when I first tried it in Vietnam. I hate the smell of raw eggs and the thought of drinking eggs made me queasy. However, I came around to it and decided this method is a perfect addition to my morning coffee. It's so special and different compared to drip coffee from a machine. First, locals prefer to use robusta coffee beans because they are more potent than arabica beans. Robusta tends to sway on the bitter side and provides a stronger source of caffeine. It's what makes Vietnamese coffee, well, Vietnamese coffee! Second, it is brewed with a phin filter, a slower percolating drip method. It takes a few minutes longer than a pour over, but trust me, it's worth the effort.

Egg Coffee

Prep Time: *5 minutes*
Total Time: *10 minutes*
Makes *1 egg coffee*

2 tablespoons **robusta coffee grounds**

About 1 cup **boiling water**

1 **large egg yolk**

1 tablespoon **condensed milk**

1   Place the coffee grounds into a phin filter cup fitted over a coffee cup. Lightly shake it to even out the grounds before you insert the gravity press. Pour 3 to 4 tablespoons of the boiling water over the grounds to wet them. Wait for it to filter down, about 30 seconds. Fill the phin filter cup to the top with boiling water, usually around $\frac{1}{3}$ cup. Put on the lid and let it slowly drip down completely, 3 to 4 minutes. If you don't have a phin filter, any espresso maker will work. You need to make $\frac{1}{2}$ cup of espresso and pour it into a coffee cup.

2   Bring a small pot of water to a bare simmer over medium heat. In a heatproof bowl that will fit over the pot of simmering water, whisk together the egg yolk and condensed milk. Place the bowl over the hot water and heat in 10-second increments, whisking vigorously on and off the heat until the egg mixture doubles in volume with an airy texture and light yellow color, 2 to 3 minutes.

3   Scoop the egg mixture over the coffee.

Soy Pudding
with Ginger Syrup

Tàu Hũ

Prep Time: *5 hours 15 minutes*

Total Time: *5 hours 15 minutes*

Makes *3 cups*

Tàu hũ, also known as tofu pudding, is a classic Vietnamese dessert. I remember always begging my mom to order it when we went on our weekly trips to the market in Vietnam.

It was magical to watch the tàu hũ lady make it in front of us. She scooped up the hot, soft tofu from a big pot. The silky, gelatinous texture with fresh ginger makes for a comforting treat. Making your own soy milk into proper tofu takes a long time, so I shortened the process with the help of gelatin. The best part about tàu hũ is that you can serve it hot, cold, or room temperature at any time of the year.

2½ tablespoon **unflavored gelatin** (1 envelope)

3 cups **plain soy milk**

2 tablespoons **rock sugar** or **sugar**

2-inch knob **fresh ginger**, peeled and julienned, reserve a few strips for garnish

1   In a small bowl, whisk the gelatin with ¼ cup of the soy milk until it dissolves. In a medium-size pot, bring the remaining soy milk to a simmer over medium heat. Whisk in the gelatin mixture. If you spot any lumps as you stir,

line a fine-mesh sieve with cheesecloth and strain the mixture into a bowl. Cool it down on the counter for 1 hour. Cover the bowl and refrigerate until the pudding is set and no longer liquidy when you shake it, 3 to 4 hours.

2   In a small saucepan, combine 1 cup water, the sugar, and ginger and cook, stirring, over medium heat until the sugar dissolves and forms a simple syrup, 2 to 3 minutes.

3   Serve the pudding cold in small dishes with ginger syrup or heat it up in the microwave for 30 seconds. Make sure each dish has a few strands of the julienned ginger on top, too.

Vietnamese Yogurt

Da Ua

Prep Time: *12 hours 15 minutes*
Total Time: *12 hours 30 minutes*
Makes *six 8-ounce jars*

One thing I love about Vietnamese yogurt, compared to American and European ones, is the subtle sweetness from incorporating condensed milk. It really helps balance out the acidity of the fermenting yogurt. If you want to amp up the tangy flavor, I suggest keeping the yogurt in the fridge for an additional 12 hours before eating it. Da ua is my mom's favorite treat because it's so easy to make and a great addition to drinks. In Vietnam, it's common to add crushed ice and milk to da ua. I've seen it scooped into limeade and smoothies, too. Since you're working with live, bacterial cultures, be sure to use sterilized jars and tools. Use a food thermometer to monitor the water temperature, because the cultures start to die at 130°F, which could leave you with a liquidy yogurt.

1   In a large bowl, whisk together the whole milk, condensed milk, hot water, and Greek yogurt until it is nice and smooth. You don't want a clumpy yogurt! Divide the mixture among 6 sterilized 8-ounce jars and screw on the lids.

2   Fill a large pot halfway with water. Bring it to a boil over high heat, then turn the heat off. Let it cool until it reaches 120°F, 5 to 10 minutes. Place the yogurt jars in the pot. Make sure the jars are covered up to their sides but not submerged in water. Use a ladle to carefully remove any excess water. Cover with the pot lid and let it sit undisturbed for 6 to 12 hours.

3   Once the yogurt has thickened, remove the jars from the water and dry off with a towel. Store in the fridge for up to 3 weeks or in the freezer for up to 2 months.

2 cups **whole milk**

1 can **condensed milk**

1 cup **hot water**

1 cup **Greek yogurt** with live cultures

Avocado Mousse

Kem Bơ

Prep Time: *5 minutes*
Total Time: *15 minutes*
Makes *a dessert for 2*

The first time I had kem bơ was when I visited Đà Lạt, Vietnam, in 2019. I served kem bơ with durian ice cream at my very first pop-up. I knew I was taking a risk. Serving durian to an American palate could be a hit or miss, but I loved the combo and decided to go with my gut. I understand durian might be an acquired taste for most people, so feel free to keep the ice cream choice simple with your favorite brand of vanilla ice cream. If you have a sweet tooth, bump up the condensed milk to 8 tablespoons. Otherwise, you can keep it at 4 for a mildly sweet milky taste.

2 **large avocados**, halved and pitted

4 to 8 tablespoons **condensed milk**

½ cup **canned coconut milk**

½ cup **durian** or **vanilla ice cream**

2 teaspoons **unsweetened shredded coconut**

1 Scoop the avocado flesh into a blender or food processor. Add 4 tablespoons of condensed milk and the coconut milk and blend on high speed. Taste and adjust the sweetness of the mousse with up to 4 more tablespoons of condensed milk, if you want. Use a spatula to scrape down the sides and blend until smooth, making sure there are NO CHUNKS!

2 Fill two 8-ounce cups with the avocado mousse, add 2 small scoops of ice cream to each, and garnish both with a healthy teaspoon of shredded coconut.

Drifting Water Dessert

Chè Trôi Nước

Prep Time: *1 hour 15 minutes*

Total Time: *3 hours*

Makes *60 to 65 balls or dessert for 12 to 20*

MUNG BEAN FILLING:

1½ cups **split yellow mung beans**

2 tablespoons **coconut milk**

2 tablespoons **sugar**, plus more to taste

RICE FLOUR DOUGH:

1¾ cups **glutinous rice flour**

1 cup warm **water**

Pinch of **kosher salt**

GINGER SYRUP:

1 cup **palm sugar**

1-inch knob **fresh ginger,** peeled and thinly sliced

2 fresh or frozen **pandan leaves,** wiped clean

FOR ASSEMBLY:

1 teaspoon **olive oil**

Sesame seeds, toasted

Chè trôi nước translates into "drifting water dessert" because of the way the rice balls float when they're finished cooking. How cute is that? These were a hit at my Lunar New Year pop-up at Madame Vo in New York City. So of course I had to add it to this cookbook! My family loves to make this dish during Lunar New Year as a reminder to let our worries and sorrows drift away. Chè trôi nước has a chewy, mochi-like exterior that works so well with sweet ginger syrup; the stuffing is a slightly sweet, creamy mung bean paste. Make sure you're using split yellow mung beans and not green mung beans, which tend to be on the earthier, less sweet side. Round up your loved ones to help with this dish. It's more efficient with an assembly line! If you venture to try it out yourself, don't let the process intimidate you. That first bite will be worth it. I promise.

1   Make the mung bean filling: Soak the mung beans in twice their volume of water for 1 hour. Drain well and rinse.

2   In a small pot, combine the mung beans and ¾ cup water. Cover and cook over medium-low heat, stirring occasionally so the beans

do not stick to the bottom, until the beans are softened and easily crushed between two fingers or with the back of a spoon, about 30 minutes.

3   Carefully mash the mung beans with a wooden spoon or masher. As you mash, slowly add the coconut milk and sugar. Adjust the seasoning with more sugar, if needed. You're looking for a clay-like consistency where you can form balls with the mixture. Once the beans are cool enough to handle, roll into balls of about 1½ teaspoons each and place in a single layer on a sheet pan. Cover with plastic wrap and set aside.

4   Make the rice flour dough: In a medium bowl, stir together the rice flour, warm water, and salt. Once it is easy to handle, knead it until it is a smooth dough. If the dough is too dry or feels crackly as you work, add more water. If the dough is too wet and sticky, add more flour.

5   Keep a small bowl of water nearby to dip your fingers as you divide the dough into the same number of portions as the number of mung bean balls you made. Roll the dough up into small, smooth balls. Cover the rice flour balls with a damp towel to prevent them from drying out.

6   Make the ginger syrup: In a medium-size pot, combine 4 cups water, the palm sugar, and ginger. Bring to a boil over medium-high heat. Reduce the heat to medium-low and simmer, stirring occasionally, until the sugar has dissolved, 2 to 3 minutes. Add the pandan leaves and keep the syrup warm over low heat.

7   To assemble: Pour the olive oil onto a sheet pan. Roll a dough ball out into a flat round big enough to cover a mung bean ball. Set a mung bean ball in the center, bring the sides of the dough up to cover the ball, and then roll it between your palms to smooth it out. Roll the formed balls on the oiled pan so they don't stick to each other.

8   Bring a large pot of water to a boil, then turn it down to a simmer over medium heat. Working in batches of 20 at a time, carefully add the rice balls to the water and boil until they float, about 3 minutes. Cook for another minute and transfer to the warm syrup. Repeat with the remaining balls in sets of 20. Once all the balls are cooked, increase the heat under the syrup to medium and simmer the rice balls in the syrup for 5 minutes.

9   Let the rice balls and syrup cool down to room temperature. Serve 3 to 5 balls in small bowls with a few spoonfuls of syrup. Garnish each bowl with a pinch of toasted sesame seeds.

Vietnamese
Banana Fritters

Chuối Chiên

Prep Time: *35 minutes*

Total Time: *1 hour 35 minutes*

Makes *10 banana fritters*

Thai bananas pack a sweeter, more concentrated flavor compared to regular bananas. You're going to want bananas that are in the middle of their ripeness, not too stiff or soft with a few brown splotches. If they're too ripe, they won't hold together when you fry them. Too firm and they will taste starchy.

The coconut sauce is optional, but I highly suggest making a batch for an extra creamy and aromatic touch against the crunch of the dessert.

1 cup **all-purpose flour**

1 tablespoon **cornstarch**

2 teaspoons **baking powder**

10 **Thai bananas**, peeled

Vegetable oil, for deep-frying (about 1 quart)

½ cup **sugar**, plus more for finishing

½ cup **Coconut Sauce** (optional; page 182)

1 In a medium bowl, combine the flour, cornstarch, baking powder, and 1½ cups water. Whisk until well combined. The mixture should feel like a loose pancake or tempura batter. Let the batter rest at room temperature for 30 minutes.

2 Press each banana into a flat oval shape by smushing it between two sheet pans. They should be a little less than ½ inch thick. Set aside.

(recipe continues)

3   Nest a wire rack in a sheet pan and set near the stove (you don't want to drain the bananas on paper towels or you'll run the risk of the sugar hardening and sticking to the paper). Pour 1 inch vegetable oil into a deep heavy pot and heat over medium-high heat to 350°F. Use a wooden chopstick to test when it's ready; it should bubble when you put it in.

4   Working with 1 or 2 bananas at a time, coat them on both sides in sugar. Quickly dip each piece into the batter, letting any excess batter drip off. Using tongs or a long spatula, carefully lower the banana pieces into the oil. Deep-fry the battered bananas until golden brown, 3 to 4 minutes. Using tongs, transfer the bananas to the wire rack. Sprinkle more sugar over the banana pieces while they're still hot. Repeat the frying with the remaining bananas.

5   Transfer the bananas to a platter. If desired, drizzle the coconut sauce over the banana fritters or transfer the sauce to a small bowl to use as dip.

I can't say enough good things about pandan. The smell and taste of pandan is so unique. Fun fact: People in Vietnam, mostly taxi drivers, put pandan leaves in their cars as an air freshener. I'm always looking for ways to experiment with it. I've tried it in jelly form, in crepes, in cupcakes, and I highlighted it in my Pandan Waffles (page 216). One day, around Valentine's Day, I saw strawberry cinnamon rolls and I thought, "What about pandan cinnamon rolls?" I scoured the Internet for recipes at the time and no luck. I had to figure it out! Pandan extract is used in baking and has an unmistakable bright green hue and a fresh, vanilla-like aroma. If you can only find pandan extract that is clear and not the signature bright green, two drops of food coloring will do the trick.

Pandan Cinnamon Rolls

Prep Time: *1 hour 40 minutes*
Total Time: *2 hours 5 minutes*
Makes *12 rolls*

COCONUT CREAM CHEESE GLAZE:

- 8 ounces **cream cheese,** at room temperature
- 2 tablespoons **unsalted butter,** at room temperature
- ½ cup **canned coconut milk**
- 1 cup **powdered sugar**

PANDAN ROLL DOUGH:

- 1 cup **whole milk**
- 1 envelope (2¼ teaspoons) **active dry yeast**
- 4 cups **all-purpose flour,** plus more for dusting
- ¼ cup **granulated sugar**
- ¼ cup (packed) **light brown sugar**
- 2 **large eggs**
- 5 tablespoons (2½ ounces) **unsalted butter,** melted
- 2 teaspoons **pandan extract**
- ½ cup **canned coconut milk**

CINNAMON SUGAR FILLING:

- 8 tablespoons (4 ounces) **unsalted butter**
- 2 tablespoons **granulated sugar**
- 2 tablespoons **light brown sugar**
- 1 tablespoon **ground cinnamon**

(recipe continues)

1   Make the cinnamon sugar filling: In a small saucepan, heat the butter over medium heat whisking constantly until it starts to foam and then subside, 4 to 6 minutes. When you see brown specks appear, take it off the heat. Transfer the butter to a heatproof bowl. Chill it in the fridge until ready to use.

2   In a small bowl, stir together the granulated sugar, brown sugar, and cinnamon. Set aside.

3   Make the coconut cream cheese glaze: In a medium bowl, whisk together the cream cheese, butter, coconut milk, and powdered sugar until smooth. Set aside.

4   Make the pandan roll dough: Warm the milk in the microwave for about 30 seconds or over low heat in a small saucepan to 100°F, about 2 minutes. Remove from the heat. Pour the yeast into the milk, stir it, and let it bloom until it starts to bubble and activate, about 5 minutes.

5   Sift the flour, granulated sugar, and brown sugar together into the bowl of a stand mixer. Add the eggs, melted butter, pandan extract, and the milk/yeast mixture. Give it a good mix on medium speed until everything comes together. The dough should feel tacky.

6   Flour a clean work surface and dump the dough out. Knead it for an additional 5 minutes until smooth. Place the dough into an oiled bowl and cover it with a kitchen towel. Let it rise until it doubles in size, 45 to 50 minutes.

7   Once the dough has risen, roll it out to a rectangle about 18 inches long and $\frac{1}{4}$ inch thick. Spread the chilled brown butter on top and sprinkle the cinnamon sugar mixture evenly over the butter.

8   Roll up the dough into a long log and then use a sharp knife, serrated knife, or unflavored dental floss to cut it crosswise into 12 pieces $1\frac{1}{2}$ inches wide. Place the rolls, cut side up and spaced $\frac{1}{2}$ inch apart in a 9 x 13–inch baking dish, and let rise for another 40 minutes.

9   Preheat the oven to 350°F.

10   Brush the coconut milk over the rolls. Bake the rolls until they have expanded and a cake tester inserted in a roll comes out clean, 25 to 30 minutes.

11   When they come out of the oven, drizzle half of the cream cheese glaze over the cinnamon rolls and spread the glaze out. Serve the rolls warm from the pan with additional glaze on the side.

Sweet Corn Pudding

Chè Bắp

Prep Time: *2 hours 15 minutes*

Total Time: *2 hours 40 minutes*

Makes *a dessert for 4*

I love incorporating pandan leaves to help accentuate the corn flavor with a grassy note. If you have yet to try sweet corn, I 100 percent urge you to look for it. It'll blow your mind with its amplified corn flavor. No matter the weather or season, you can eat sweet corn pudding hot or cold.

1. Slice the corn kernels from the cob, then break the cobs in half. Set the kernels aside.

2. In a small saucepan, combine the cobs, 4 cups water, and the pandan leaves and bring to a boil over high heat. Reduce the heat to medium-low and simmer for 10 minutes.

3. In a small bowl, soak the tapioca pearls in enough hot water to cover by $\frac{1}{2}$ inch. Stir and keep them submerged as they bloom.

4. Carefully remove the cobs and pandan leaves from the saucepan and discard. Add the corn kernels, sugar, and salt and give it a good whisk to combine. Simmer until the salt and sugar are dissolved, about 5 minutes. Skim off any foam.

5. Drain the bloomed tapioca and add to the pan. Simmer until the tapioca floats, skimming any foam that gathers around the edges, about 3 minutes. Transfer the pudding to a heatproof bowl and let it cool for 10 minutes. Cover and refrigerate for at least 2 hours before serving.

6. Serve the chè bắp in small bowls with a generous tablespoon of sweet coconut sauce and a pinch of toasted sesame seeds on each.

2 ears **sweet corn,** shucked

4 fresh or frozen **pandan leaves,** wiped clean

$\frac{1}{2}$ cup **mini tapioca pearls**

Hot water

$\frac{1}{2}$ cup **sugar**

Pinch of **kosher salt**

1 cup **Coconut Sauce** (page 182)

Sesame seeds, toasted

Chè Thái

I have fond memories of my mom making chè Thái for large parties and family gatherings. The key to success with this fruit salad is to drain off all the canned fruit syrup. I like to use Aroy-D brand canned fruits. The syrup from canned fruit has a lot of sugar, which makes it difficult for you to control the sweetness level later. Sometimes canned fruit syrup will also leave a metallic taste in your mouth—that's a flavor we want to stay away from, especially in desserts. I suggest using rock sugar rather than regular sugar to avoid a grainy finish. Rock sugar has a more mellow flavor, which leaves more room to adjust the sweetness level. Try chè Thái if you're craving something sweet but you're pressed for time and want a quick treat from the pantry.

Prep Time: *45 minutes*

Total Time: *1 hour*

Makes *a dessert for 8*

1 (20-ounce) **can jackfruit in syrup,** drained

1 (5-ounce) **can lychees,** drained

1 (20-ounce) **can rambutan,** drained

1 (20-ounce) **can green grass jelly**

1 (20-ounce) **jar coconut jelly** or **nata de coco cubes,** drained

½ cup **rock sugar** or **granulated sugar**

½ cup **pomegranate seeds**

1 cup **canned coconut milk**

1 cup **half-and-half**

1   Rinse all of the canned fruits and jellies in a colander. Cut the jackfruit into strips. Cut the lychee and rambutan in half. Slice the grass jelly into ½-inch cubes.

2   In a small pot, heat 1 cup water over medium-low heat. Add the rock sugar and stir until it has dissolved, 2 to 3 minutes. Take the pot off the heat and let it cool for 10 minutes.

3   In a large bowl, combine all the fruits, the pomegranate seeds, jellies, coconut milk, and half-and-half. Mix it well and add the simple syrup a little at a time. Taste as you go and base it on the sweetness level that you want.

4   Cover the fruit cocktail and refrigerate for at least 30 minutes to chill before serving it in small bowls.

Three Color Dessert

Chè Ba Màu

Prep Time: *3 hours*

Total Time: *4 hours 20 minutes*

Makes *a dessert for 8*

Summers in California can be so painfully hot. What better way to cool off in the sun than with an ice slush? Shaved ice from a machine is ideal for chè ba màu, but don't go out of your way to get your hands on one. Crushed ice from the freezer is much easier! Chè ba màu is also known as "three color dessert" and is made of three major components: bouncy jelly, sweet soft beans, and rich coconut sauce. That's just the beginning, too. It's an exciting dish to eat with a spoon and a fun medium to play around with. Feel free to experiment with fruits like lychee, mango, strawberries, or durian (as they do in Vietnam).

PANDAN JELLY:

4 fresh or frozen **pandan leaves,** wiped clean and roughly chopped

$2\frac{1}{2}$ tablespoons **unflavored gelatin** (1 envelope)

2 to 3 tablespoons **sugar**

MUNG BEANS:

1 cup **split yellow mung beans**

Pinch of **kosher salt**

$\frac{1}{2}$ cup **canned coconut milk**

RED KIDNEY BEANS:

1 cup **sugar**

1 (15.5-ounce) **can red kidney beans, drained and rinsed**

FOR SERVING:

4 cups **crushed** or **shaved ice**

$\frac{1}{2}$ cup **Coconut Sauce** (page 182)

1   Make the pandan jelly: In a blender, combine the chopped pandan leaves and $\frac{1}{2}$ cup water and blend until smooth and bright green. Strain the fresh pandan extract through a fine-mesh sieve into a bowl.

2   In a small pot, bring 2 cups water to a simmer over medium heat. Whisk the gelatin into the hot water along with the pandan extract and 2 tablespoons of sugar. Taste and add an additional tablespoon of sugar if you like it sweeter. Whisk the mixture until the gelatin and sugar dissolve, 1 to 2 minutes. Pour the mixture into a small $2\frac{1}{2}$ cup jelly mold, quarter sheet pan, or bowl. Cover and refrigerate until

it turns into firm jelly, about 3 hours. Once the jelly is firm, slice it into $\frac{1}{2}$-inch by 2-inch strips with $\frac{1}{4}$-inch thickness.

3 Cook the mung beans: Rinse the yellow mung beans and drain. In a small pot, combine the mung beans and $1\frac{1}{2}$ cups water and bring to a simmer over medium-high heat. Once it bubbles, reduce the heat to medium-low, cover, and simmer until tender and easily smashed between two fingers, about 30 minutes.

4 Remove from the heat and mush the mung beans together with a fork or masher. Stir in the salt and coconut milk to loosen the consistency. Set the mung beans aside to cool.

5 Prepare the kidney beans: In a small pot, stir 1 cup water and the sugar over medium heat until the sugar dissolves, 1 to 2 minutes. Cook it until it's nice and thick but pourable, 6 to 10 minutes longer. It should be a little under a cup.

6 Place the rinsed kidney beans in a heatproof container. Pour the simple syrup over the beans. Let it soak and come to room temperature until you're ready to put the dessert together.

7 To serve: Place $\frac{1}{2}$ cup crushed ice at the bottom of each of eight tall 10-ounce glasses. Top the ice with 3 tablespoons of each component in this order: red kidney beans, mung beans, and pandan jelly. Finish each glass with a drizzle of coconut sauce.

Pandan Waffles

Prep Time: *1 hour 20 minutes*
Total Time: *1 hour 50 minutes*
Makes *8 waffles*

Have you ever heard of baking cookies right before you welcome visitors into your home, so your place smells like freshly baked cookies once they walk in? Whatever your answer is, I can do you one better. Make these pandan waffles before company arrives and they'll be impressed by the smell alone. The pandan aroma will waft throughout your kitchen for hours and you might just prefer this rich, coconutty smell over lighting a candle. Aromatherapy aside, pandan waffles are a classic Vietnamese dessert and they're almost effortless to make. If you can source fresh or frozen pandan leaves, please get them for this recipe! Real pandan leaves have a more intense, vibrant flavor than their artificial extract counterpart. No syrup is needed; top the waffles with a scoop of your favorite ice cream and enjoy!

(recipe continues)

8 fresh or frozen **pandan leaves**, wiped clean and chopped

½ cup **water**

1 (13.5-ounce) **can coconut cream** or **full-fat coconut milk**

3 **large eggs**

1 tablespoon **vegetable oil**

2 cups **tapioca flour** or **starch**

1 cup **sugar**

½ cup **rice flour**

½ cup **all-purpose flour**

2 teaspoons **baking powder**

Pinch of **kosher salt**

Cooking spray

Ice cream or **Vietnamese iced coffee** (optional; for how to brew, see Egg Coffee, page 199)

1 In a blender, combine the pandan leaves and the water and blend until there are no big pieces. Strain the pulp through a fine-mesh sieve or cheesecloth into a bowl, pressing the pulp to extract the pandan flavor and color.

2 In a large bowl, combine the pandan extract, coconut cream, eggs, and vegetable oil, whisking until everything is well combined.

3 In another large bowl, mix the tapioca flour, sugar, rice flour, all-purpose flour, baking powder, and salt. Sift the dry ingredients into the wet ingredients and fold it to incorporate, do not overmix. Let the batter rest at room temperature for at least 1 hour. (By the way, at this point, it can be stored in the fridge for up to 1 week.)

4 When the waffle batter is ready, heat up a waffle maker. Mist cooking spray onto the iron and make the waffles according to the manufacturer's instructions.

5 Serve the waffles on plates with a scoop of ice cream or a side of Vietnamese iced coffee (if using), or my favorite . . . just by itself.

Pandan Honeycomb Mochi Cake

Prep Time: *45 minutes*
Total Time: *1 hour 45 minutes*
Makes *an 8-inch cake*

The name of this dish is slightly misleading. Honeycomb cake is a well-known dessert in Vietnamese cuisine and is named for its honeycomb-like interior once it is baked. Sorry, there isn't any honey in this recipe (but I won't blame you for adding honey as a topping!). The crumb is spongy and fluffy while the outside is a crumbly, golden-brown crust—achieved without all-purpose flour! Source a pandan extract that is green to achieve the rich, brilliant deep green that it is famous for. Pandan is a strong aromatic on its own, but when you pair it with coconut milk, you'll be rewarded with an unbelievable blend of milky, sweet, and airy sensations in one bite.

Cooking spray

1 (13.5-ounce) **can coconut milk**

1 cup **sugar**

3 tablespoons **coconut oil**

Pinch of **kosher salt**

2 cups **tapioca starch** or **flour**

½ cup **rice flour**

1 tablespoon **baking powder**

6 **large eggs**

1 teaspoon **pandan extract**

1   Preheat the oven to 350°F and remove any racks above the middle rack. Mist an 8-inch cake pan or Bundt pan with cooking spray.

2   In a saucepan, combine the coconut milk, sugar, coconut oil, and salt. Bring to a simmer over medium heat and stir until the sugar is dissolved, 2 to 3 minutes. Once the sugar and coconut oil dissolve, set the coconut mixture aside off the heat to cool.

3   Sift the tapioca starch, rice flour, and baking powder into a bowl and stir it with a spatula.

4   To the cooled coconut mixture, add the eggs and the pandan extract. Use a spatula to barely combine it, do not overmix! Add the coconut/egg mixture to the flour mixture. Use a spatula to fold it and bring it together gently. Pass the mixture through a mesh sieve to get rid of any lumps.

5   Pour the batter into the prepared pan. Bake on the middle rack until the top inflates and toasts to a light brown, about 45 minutes.

6   Let the cake cool for 30 minutes before slicing and serving on small plates.

Umami Chocolate Chip Cookies

Prep Time: *1 hour 15 minutes*
Total Time: *1 hour 45 minutes*
Makes *12 cookies*

Using fish sauce in a cookie recipe sounds crazy, I admit it. My umami chocolate chip cookies are definitely one of the riskier desserts in this cookbook, but hear me out! If you're curious and adventurous enough, you'll be rewarded with cookies that appear simple but are complex when you take a bite. The undercurrent of fish sauce adds a potent but pleasant salty counter to the dark chocolate and vanilla. I always chill my dough in the fridge overnight because the longer the fat in the cookies remains solid, the less it spreads out when it bakes. You're left with a satisfying, layered bite.

---

8 tablespoons (4 ounces) **unsalted butter**

1½ cups **all-purpose flour**

½ teaspoon **baking soda**

½ cup (packed) **dark brown sugar**

½ cup **granulated sugar**

1 **large egg**

1 **large egg yolk**

1 tablespoon **fish sauce**

2 teaspoons **vanilla extract**

3½ ounces **dark chocolate**, roughly chopped

Flaky salt (optional), for topping

1 In a small saucepan, melt the butter over medium heat and whisk it constantly for 4 to 6 minutes. It will start to foam and subside. When you see brown specks appear, take it off the heat.

2 In a large bowl, sift together the flour and baking soda. In another bowl, whisk together the browned butter, the dark brown and granulated sugars, the whole egg, egg yolk, fish sauce, and vanilla.

3   Pour half of the flour mixture into the butter/
    sugar mixture and mix well with a spatula.
    Once everything is combined, stir in the other
    half of the flour mixture; do not overmix. Fold
    the dark chocolate into the dough. Cover the
    dough with plastic wrap and refrigerate for
    1 hour or overnight.

4   Preheat the oven to 350°F. Line two baking
    sheets with parchment paper.

5   Use a 1½-ounce ice cream scooper to scoop the
    cookies onto the sheets spacing them 2 inches
    apart to give the cookies enough room to
    expand.

6   Bake the cookies until they have spread out
    and look golden brown in the center and along
    the edges, 10 to 15 minutes. Sprinkle a light
    amount of flaky salt on the cookies while they
    are warm—this step is optional, but it's bomb,
    so try it. Let the cookies cool for 5 minutes
    on the baking sheet before transferring to a
    platter.

7   Store covered at room temperature for up to
    1 week.

Asian Banana Bread

Prep Time: *40 minutes*

Total Time: *1 hour 45 minutes*

Makes *a 10-inch Bundt or an 8½-inch loaf*

I was eating a Thai banana one day and wondered how it would taste in a slice of banana bread. I tested it out and, whoa, it was way better than I had expected, a true delight for the taste buds! Thai bananas are also known as apple bananas or *pisang raja*, which means "king banana." They're sweeter and creamier than regular bananas, which makes them even more suited for this task. The texture of my bread is moist and tender with a complex perfume of caramel and vanilla. For crunch, I added walnuts and a finish of fragrant sesame seeds. You'll wonder how you've gone through life without my recipe.

Cooking spray

8 ripe **Thai bananas**

8 tablespoons (4 ounces) **unsalted butter**, melted

½ cup (packed) **light brown sugar**

½ cup **granulated sugar**

2 **large eggs**

1 teaspoon **vanilla extract**

½ teaspoon **sesame oil**

½ cup **semisweet chocolate chips**

½ cup **chopped walnuts**

1½ cups **all-purpose flour**

1 tablespoon **cornstarch**

1 teaspoon **baking soda**

½ teaspoon **baking powder**

½ teaspoon **ground cinnamon**

½ teaspoon **kosher salt**

1 tablespoon **black and white sesame seeds**, toasted

1   Preheat the oven to 350°F. Mist a 10-cup Bundt pan or an 8½-inch loaf pan with cooking spray.

2   Mash the bananas in a large bowl. Add the melted butter, the light brown and granulated sugars, the eggs, vanilla, sesame oil, chocolate chips, and walnuts and whisk it all together.

3   In a separate large bowl, whisk together the flour, cornstarch, baking soda, baking powder, cinnamon, and salt. Add the flour mixture to the butter/sugar mixture and fold it gently until all the flour is combined.

4   Pour the batter into the prepared pan. If you're using a loaf pan, sprinkle the sesame seeds on

top. If you're using a Bundt pan, reserve the sesame seeds for coating the bread afterward.

5 Bake until the bread has risen and lightly browned, 40 to 50 minutes. To test if it is done, stick a skewer or cake tester in a few spots. It should come out clean with no wet dough.

6 Let the banana bread cool in the pan for 30 minutes. Run a table knife along the edges of the bread to loosen it, being careful not to cut the bread itself. Unmold the Bundt or loaf pan onto a platter and slice into 1-inch pieces.

Thanks

I want to take a moment to express my heartfelt appreciation to everyone who has been a part of my journey in writing this cookbook. First, I would like to thank Ray Hughes and the RHM team for keeping me in check and on track with the project. Their support and guidance have been invaluable in bringing this cookbook to life.

I also want to express my gratitude to my mom, whose love for cooking and dedication to feeding me with flavors that bind me closer to my roots has inspired me throughout this project. Every single meal she has ever cooked for me has been a lesson in love and passion for food.

I would like to thank Kevin, whose ways of cooking and advice have been a huge inspiration to me. His culinary skills and passion for food have taught me so much about the art of cooking.

A big shout-out to my co-writer Jenn de la Vega, who has been a guiding light and held my hand throughout this journey of writing a book, which was new to me. Her expertise and support have been instrumental in bringing this project to fruition.

I am grateful to Liz Parker, my literary agent, for believing in me and championing my story. Her support and dedication have been invaluable to me.

I want to thank Justin Schwartz, executive editor of Simon Element, an imprint of Simon & Schuster, for believing in me and providing me with this incredible opportunity to share my love for food with the world.

To my friends and support system, thank you for being there for me in moments of distress and for your words of encouragement. Your unwavering support has kept me going.

And last, but certainly not least, I want to thank every single person who has been with me on this journey. This is another huge milestone that my supporters have made happen, and I could not have done it without you. Thank you all from the bottom of my heart.

Index

chives, in Bomb-Ass Ranch, 178

Chocolate Chip Cookies, Umami, 220–221

chocolate chips, in Asian Banana Bread,
    222–223

Chopped (competition show), 152

Chuối Chiên (Vietnamese Banana Fritters), 206–
    208

cilantro leaves

    Bánh Canh Cua (Crab Udon), 132–133

    Beet Soup, 123

    Bò Kho "Birria" Tacos, 165–167

    Bún Chả (Vermicelli Bowl), 46–47

    Canh Khổ Qua (Bitter Melong Soup),
        128–129

    Canh Trúng Cà Chua (Sour Tomato Egg Drop
        Soup), 120

    Crab Fried Rice, 44–45

    Gỏi Gá (Chicken Slaw), 107

    Kevin's Phở, 138–141

    Mién Xào Cua (Crab Cellophane Noodles),
        98–99

    Seafood Boil Pasta, 82–83

    Squash Soup, 124

    Xíu Mại (Pork Meatballs), 72–73

Cinnamon Rolls, Pandan, 209–211

cinnamon sticks

    Bò Kho "Birria" Tacos, 165–167

    Kevin's Phở, 138–141

    Lemongrass Chili Oil, 186–187

Clam Curry, Spicy, 152–153

Clear Dumplings (Bánh Bột Lọc), 62–63

coconut cream, in Pandan Waffles, 216–218

coconut jelly, in Chè Thái (Mixed Fruit Cocktail
    Dessert), 213

coconut milk

    about, 7

    Bánh Xèo (Vietnamese Crepes), 50–52

Cà Ri Gà (Chicken Curry), 38–39

Chè Ba Màu (Three Color Dessert), 214–215

Chè Thái (Mixed Fruit Cocktail Dessert), 213

Chè Trôi Nước (Drifting Water Dessert),
    Coconut Sauce, 182

Kem Bơ (Avocado Mousse), 202

Pandan Cinnamon Rolls, 209–211

Pandan Honeycomb Mochi Cake, 219

Pandan Waffles, 216–218

Peanut Sauce, 179

Spicy Clam Curry, 152–153

Coconut Sauce

    Chè Ba Màu (Three Color Dessert), 214–215

    Chè Bắp (Sweet Corn Pudding), 212

    Chuối Chiên (Vietnamese Banana Fritters),
        206–208

    recipe, 182

coconut, shredded, in Kem Bơ (Avocado Mousse),
    202

coconut soda

    Bánh Xèo (Vietnamese Crepes), 50–52

    Cá Kho (Braised Catfish), 35–37

    Thịt Kho (Braised Pork), 42–43

coffee

    Egg Coffee, 199

    Vietnamese Coffee Crème Brûlée,
        112–114

Cơm Tam (Grilled Pork Chops Broken Rice Plate),
    53–55

condensed milk

    Da Ua (Vietnamese Yogurt), 201

    Egg Coffee, 199

    Kem Bơ (Avocado Mousse), 202

condiments

    Lemongrass Chili Oil, 186–187

    Lemongrass Satê, 181

    Scallion Oil, 177

    Sweet Chili Sauce, 185

SIMON
ELEMENT

An Imprint of Simon & Schuster, LLC
1230 Avenue of the Americas
New York, NY 10020

Copyright © 2024 by Twaydabae Inc.
Photography © 2024 by Andrew Bui

Food Stylist: Erika Joyce
Food Stylist Assistant: Aaron Meftah
Prop Stylist: Casha Doemland
Prop Stylist Assistant: Cinthia Artiaga

First Simon Element hardcover edition September 2024

SIMON ELEMENT is a trademark of Simon & Schuster, LLC

Simon & Schuster: Celebrating 100 Years of Publishing in 2024

For information about special discounts for bulk purchases, please contact Simon & Schuster Special Sales at 1-866-506-1949 or business@ simonandschuster.com.
The Simon & Schuster Speakers Bureau can bring authors to your live event. For more information or to book an event, contact the Simon & Schuster Speakers Bureau at 1-866-248-3049 or visit our website at www.simonspeakers.com.

Interior design by Jen Wang

Manufactured in China

10 9 8 7 6 5 4 3 2 1

Library of Congress Cataloging-in-Publication Data has been applied for.

ISBN 978-1-6680-0380-0
ISBN 978-1-6680-0381-7 (ebook)